How to
Speak
and
Write
Persuasively

ROBERT VICAR

KOGAN
PAGE

First published in 1994

The masculine pronoun has been used throughout this book. This stems from a desire to avoid ugly and cumbersome language, and no discrimination, prejudice or bias is intended.

Kogan Page Limited
120 Pentonville Road
London N1 9JN

British Library Cataloguing in Publication Data

A CIP record for this book is available from the British Library.

ISBN 0 7494 1328 X

Typeset by DP Photosetting, Aylesbury, Bucks
Printed in England by Clays Ltd, St Ives plc

How to
Speak
and
Write
Persuasively

The author

The Author was educated at Stonyhurst College in Lancashire, from where he joined the Royal Canadian Air Force, serving as an Aircrew Navigator.

After returning to the UK, his total business career has been involved with marketing and selling, both in service organisations and in capital equipment, some twenty years being spent with an associate company of Taylor Woodrow Limited where he served in the capacity of Sales Manager and Director, being directly involved in the recruitment and training of the sales force under his control. He has extensive experience both in personal selling in the field and also in Sales Management, and well appreciates the many problems facing both new and qualified sales professionals in the field who often have to discover, by harsh experience, the right and the wrong way of becoming a real sales expert.

Apart from writing sales training manuals, Robert Vicar now operates his own company, selling specifically to the construction and allied industries, a market which he still regards as one of the hardest training grounds for any new salesperson.

He is also the author of *Prospecting For Customers, One Foot On The Management Ladder* and *First Division Selling*, all published by Kogan Page.

Robert Vicar
1994

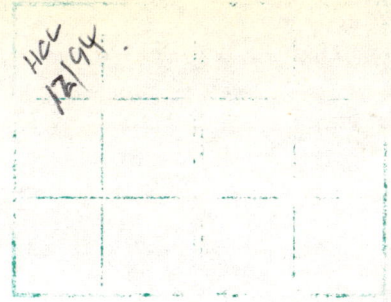

HCL
12/94.

Contents

Preface

This book, unlike many, is not just about public speaking, although that aspect inevitably comes into it, but it *is* about speaking in public in any situation. It is about improving your ability to sound convincing to others, and being clearly understood by others. The advice in this book concerns communication, in all its forms, and is about a skill which can be both learnt and improved. It is also about a skill which now forms an increasingly smaller part of the school curriculum with the result that fewer people, both in business and in their everyday lives, are able to express themselves clearly and persuasively.

However, the rules for general conversation are very similar to those for public speaking and a great deal of the advice given for one applies equally to the other. In fact, over the last few generations, the old style of public speaking, which once differed totally from the way people normally conversed, has now gone, and in public places, and in the media, we prefer to hear a more informal presentation and production.

Conversation is not just speaking. Writing is not just setting down words. Both are a part of communication between two or more human beings and involve getting a message across in the most convincing and persuasive way possible. Words certainly play their part, but more important is our own ability to appreciate how those words hit their target and what reaction they get.

We communicate in many ways, by exchanging ideas and in some cases by placing our own ideas on top of those of others. Sometimes we communicate by saying nothing at all, by a shrug of the shoulders, by eye contact or even the lack of it, and sometimes by turning away: 'body language'. Even slamming a door is a method of communication, albeit a negative one. This resort to basic responses such as door slamming to make a point occurs solely because a person may have no other means of communication at their disposal; it is often seen in children, for example. It can be the reason why inexperienced business people often destroy the effect of what they *have* said by the careless manner in which they present it.

There is such a wide difference between those who communicate effectively and those who do not, that the skill of ensuring that our words are not wasted is important if the rest of what we learn about selling is to be used effectively. If we cannot communicate; if we are abrasive; if we do not have a proper command of language; or if we convey a picture other than the one we are aiming for; we will always find it difficult to be successful in business since, however good our ideas, we will be unable to pass them across to others. Both in business and our private lives, we need to relate to others and they to us. We need to influence others and ensure they come to us to hear our opinions and our views. But in any conversation, both sides need to have the same picture of what has been said. For that we need good communication and that means good conversation.

If we merely wish to send out information, then the rules are simple: *Say the minimum and say it clearly*. Beyond that, if information is the only criterion we need say no more. But rarely is conversation used just for that purpose (and often not even for that); its function of establishing a rapport between two people is often as important as the detail of what is actually said. Effective conversation, in any context, *must* fulfil three basic functions:

- it must be an interchange of ideas;

- it must make the listener *hear* what we say; and

- *it must make the listener be equally receptive to it.*

This means establishing a skill in presenting the words that we say, in using words which have originality and colour, and in making the composition of our speech attractive and rhythmical.

It also means training ourselves to listen. That listening becomes most important in our work and our business, not just when attending meetings but also when dealing with our superiors and our subordinates. To succeed in any business, we *must* get the listening part right. Most people are bad listeners, which means that even when we become skilful at it ourselves, we are still dealing most of our time with people who are not listening properly to us. Listening is not just hearing the words – we all do that – it is also the interpretation of those words and our response to them. We are, of course, always tuned in to our own specific topics and automatically accept those more readily than those in which we are less interested. All of us have, when in a large room, tuned in to a group ten feet away whose subject is on our wavelength whilst ignoring the person immediately in front of us. If we really *want* to listen to the person with us, we must make a conscious effort to get ourselves on to his or her wavelength before we are really part of the conversation. Everyone, particularly those in business, needs to practise this art before they are successful at it.

Communication remains a much neglected subject. With the current emphasis on degree-learnt knowledge, it is probably true that less and less importance is placed on communicating that skill to others, and as a result, our ability to use our own language is given a lower priority than technical disciplines. This book attempts to redress that balance and to show how easy it can be to improve our conversational and persuasive skills, and how that improvement can be an essential asset in making better use of all the other talents that we have chosen to use in our careers.

Robert Vicar
1994

Acknowledgements

Acknowledgement must be made to all those, both famous and also less well known, whose apt words have occasionally been quoted in the text and chapter headings of this book. My only wish is that I had thought of them first myself.

Many of the quotations have been taken from various anthologies and I should like to acknowledge the assistance of the compilers of the following collections whose work made the finding of appropriate quotations somewhat easier.

The Bloomsbury Thematic Dictionary of Quotations compiled by the Bloomsbury Publishing Co, London 1V 5DE.

The Speaker Digest of Business Quotations compiled by Rolfe White and published by W Foulsham and Co Ltd, Slough, SL1 4JH.

A Treasury of Business Quotations compiled by Michael C Thomsett and published by St James Press, London W1P 9FA.

The Speaker's Handbook of Epigrams and Witticisms compiled by Herbert V Prochnow and published by A Thomas and Co Ltd, Blackpool, Lancashire.

The Oxford Dictionary of Modern Quotations edited by Tony Augarde and published by Oxford University Press, Walton Street, Oxford, OX2 6DP.

A Dictionary of Twentieth Century Quotations compiled by Nigel Rees and published by Fontana Paperbacks, 8 Grafton Street, London W1X 3LA.

The Penguin Dictionary of Quotations compiled by J M and M J Cohen and published by Omega Books, 1 West Street, Ware, Hertfordshire.

The Fitzhenry and Whiteside Book of Quotations published in Toronto, Canada.

The Manager's Book of Quotations compiled by Lewis D Eigen and Jonathan P Siegel and published by The Quotations Corporation, 12612 St James Road, Rockville, MD 20850 USA.

Also my acknowledgements to the following:
Robert Frost; Robert Benchley; A A Milne; O Henry; Winston Churchill; Irvin S Cobb; George Bernard Shaw; G K Chesterton; Norman R Augustine; Elizabeth Bowen; Dorothy Sarnoff; Charles Reade; James Thurber; Dr Samuel Johnson; Blaise Pascal; Ralph Waldo Emerson; and Walter Bagehot.

I

Getting the message across

Half the world is composed of people who have something to say and can't, and the other half of people who have nothing to say and keep on saying it.

Robert Frost, *quoted in Kansas City Star,* 14 July 1977

Speaking well is not merely a question of learning a correct vocabulary and then using it in an acceptable sequence; nor is it even achieving a 'melody' so that the words are pleasant to listen to, although certainly both those attributes must make listening easier. It certainly *is* a policy of making your presentation, whether in a small group or to a wider audience, interesting *in itself* without that quality being necessarily related solely to the content of what is being said. Language must be simple and easily understood. That means avoiding ill-constructed and ugly sentences, and it means developing the use of graphic, colourful words; words which portray, as best they can, the image you have in your own mind.

Everyday conversation is basically instinctive. Generally it needs little planning and whilst we are among those who speak the same language as ourselves, we get by, some of us better than others. However, if we move out of those familiar surroundings, perhaps to a foreign country or into an unfamiliar group of people, we discover that our natural conversation is not good enough and the standards that were previously acceptable are now inadequate for our new environment. It is not simply that our conversational abilities are limited, but they are limited *in certain circumstances*. There are few of us who would claim to be at home in every possible circumstance we are likely to find ourselves, however, if we can increase our communication skills, we can be confident of being able to meet most situations at least half way.

BECOMING MORE ACCEPTABLE

This means deleting the distractions that limit our abilities, whether those distractions are vocal or physical. It may mean modifying accents or dialects if either of those are heavy or block understanding. It may mean adjusting an exaggerated tone, smoothing an abrasive manner or even varying a monotonous pitch, any of which may prevent an audience listening to you. It may mean increasing a limited vocabulary so that what you have to say is presented in a more acceptable and interesting way.

It may be a simple matter of balancing what you have to say so that your whole conversation is well presented and rhythmic in itself. The meaning should certainly be clearly understood by your listeners. An erratic and stumbling conversation is often interpreted as meaning something totally different. Sympathy may be construed as interference. Humour may be taken 'in the wrong way'. These misunderstandings in conversation create a lack of confidence in our speaking and are largely the result of not having thought out what we wanted to say.

INCREASE YOUR SELF-CONFIDENCE

The barriers to good speaking are probably different for everyone but if one factor stands at the root of all the others, it is *lack of confidence*. Once we have confidence, for example, that the vocabulary we have is adequate for what we have to say (whether or not it is better than that of someone else), then we have the ability to improve on other aspects of our presentation. If we can be sure that our dialect does not detract from being understood, then we can concentrate on the words that we choose. If we are constantly aware that either of those presents a problem then, even though our subject knowledge may be impeccable, we will have little confidence in our ability to transmit that knowledge with conviction to someone else.

Understanding how to speak correctly starts with an understanding of how other successful people both speak and write. It is no coincidence that the majority of those in the public eye who speak well and with conviction are also avid readers and listeners and are people who have succeeded in recognising in others the style they try to cultivate for themselves. How many politicians do you disagree with, who are nevertheless entertaining to listen to and who have learnt to enthral their audiences without necessarily securing their agreement? One only has to listen to *Any Questions* on the BBC to see that the controversial and articulate speakers are also those who are regularly invited to return to the programme. Winston Churchill himself had many detractors for most of his career, and, between the wars, probably had more people disagreeing with him than supporting him, but whether what he had to say was acceptable or not, few would deny his ability and skill to present views in an authoritative and magnetic way. Churchill *learnt* how to speak well: he spent hours training his voice and presentation so that the content of his speech, whatever it was, became more difficult to refute. That is what good speaking (or writing) is about; good speaking is a rare natural talent and even the most talented will admit to having learnt by the imitation of others, and not without a great deal of hard work.

PERFECT YOUR PRESENTATION

Equally there are those, some who possibly represent the political parties we each voted for, who cannot say *anything* without arousing irritation and fury. They make hard work of the job of promoting what might well be a logical and convincing argument simply because they have not learnt the art of presenting it in an acceptable way. A convincing argument must be linked with a persuasive personality, and this means both the words that are said and the manner in which they are presented.

Consider how much more effective many of the real reformers of this day, amongst them many politicians and Trade Union Officials, would be if they could also present their cases clearly and articulately. Sadly, few believe that the presentation demands as much preparation as the content and they consequently fail to achieve the impact that the subject demands. Conversely, many who have unacceptable views succeed in getting others to listen to them solely as a result of the power of oratory at their command. Adolf Hitler's asset was not solely what he said, but his extraordinary command of the audience that he was addressing. Conversation in everyday life is no different and needs the same attention to detail and method to secure what we want. Fortunately this can be acquired, and if you improve your style of spoken English, the improvement in your written style will certainly follow.

Good speaking cannot be taught easily through a correspondence course although I am well aware that there are many such courses on the market, all claiming remarkable success in minimal time. What these courses *can* teach you is the correct use of grammar and indeed the extension of your vocabulary although even those assets will rely essentially on you spending a lot of time on the necessary groundwork. I believe that by following the guidelines in this book, that groundwork will be done for you.

LEARN FROM OTHERS

Putting together the basis of your speaking must necessarily be the result of a slower process over a long period and involves absorption of the writings and the speech of others, so that you learn to recognise and avoid faults in your own repertoire. If you react correctly to the person who says 'I'll have two of them doughnuts,' and know that such a link up of words is both ungrammatical and ugly, you will eventually find, in your own usage of English, that substituting 'those' for 'them' would become automatic. In such a simple example you might well believe that the difference is of no consequence since either way you will probably get the two doughnuts you want, but if you are also trying to convince your listener of your education, or the style and quality of your background, then by using the word 'them' in this context you will have done the complete opposite. That is where the oft-quoted argument in favour of achieving your immediate objective, by whatever method, falls down, as it disregards all other aspects of what conversation is meant to be. I hope you are not one of the proponents of this argument, since your aim in life is not merely to convey what you need to say, but to use your conversation to encourage your listener to form the right opinions about you.

It is indeed quite remarkable that in all the foreign languages we study at school, and subsequently, we are required to speak to a certain conversational standard, and yet, when studying English, the concentration and priority is on grammar and vocabulary, with little attention paid to the way or style in which we use that vocabulary to express ourselves. This is not intended to be a book on grammar, but it *will* be an attempt to improve your method of getting the message across and in a more persuasive manner, even for those with only limited knowledge of the English language. It will also encourage you to use the grammar and style of others to highlight the faults in your own use of the English language.

SPEAK AND BE JUDGED!

What you will learn are the skills which will secure advantages far in excess of the simple (I use the word advisedly) asset of being able to formulate words and sentences in the right order. You will learn how to handle situations which might otherwise leave you struggling for the right way to express yourself. You will find that the type of English you use influences the reliance people are prepared to place on your opinions, and you will find that speaking forcefully and with conviction, and having the knowledge that you can do so whenever you wish, gives you an enhanced confidence in yourself and your own abilities.

Remember that slovenly speech usually indicates a poor education. This is not in any way a criticism in itself since at an early stage in life we may not necessarily get the advantages of a good education, and anyway, our environment probably has more to do with the way we speak than anything else. However most of us will, if we can, improve on the teaching of our early years, and it is foolish to display ignorance when we do not have to do so.

IMPROVE YOUR IMAGE

There are indeed many ways you can develop this ability to improve the way others see you and whilst vocabulary and the combination of words you use is not to be dismissed there will also be many approaches that you will be looking at so that you are listened to instead of being merely heard. That is the skill of talking with conviction so you are better placed to convince others and is a vital skill for any professional person to acquire.

How you act and how you display emotion also tells as much about your true feelings as does what you say. The person who says 'No, you haven't offended me' may well be the same person who, through the expression on his face or the tension in his hands, tells you that is *just* what you have done. Your body language can just as easily weaken what you have said as strengthen it, and the skilful choice of that body language is as important as the words you express. A good salesman, and indeed a good conversationalist, will always recognise signs of inattention or annoyance in his audience, either through their posture or expression, but he should also remember that an astute listener will be doing the same with him.

It is also well to remember that a great deal of our ability to speak with conviction is influenced by our personal chemistry. Few of us have not experienced meeting someone (of either sex) with whom we have felt an instant rapport. A relationship exists immediately, and makes talking and listening a far easier operation. It is this kind of relationship which we all try to encourage in our everyday lives. In a sales environment it is called empathy, and contrary to popular belief, it *can* be developed. Indeed in conversation of any sort you will find that you are more interested in others when they are interested in you; the whole link between two people implies a mutual two-way flow of interest and involvement. One-way communication, especially in a business situation, is heading for failure.

CHECKLIST

- Language must be simple and easily understood.
- Self-confidence is the key to persuasive speaking.
- Clear presentation will also make you speak with authority.
- Recognise and avoid the communication errors of others.
- Develop empathy with your listeners.

2

Articulation and rhythm in your speaking

It was one of those plays in which all the actors unfortunately enunciated very clearly.

Robert Benchley, US Humorist and Drama Critic (1889–1945)

S adly, correct use of the voice (except possibly in drama school) is rarely taught in our colleges and schools, and children will normally adopt the same standards as the environment in which they live. Those who go to private schools are not necessarily taught more thoroughly than those who do not, but the type of surroundings in which they work and play automatically encourages them to match up to the standard of their peers, and which becomes the norm for themselves. Similarly those who pass their time among friends who speak in a slovenly way will usually adopt the same habits and will probably be unaware, until they go out into the wider world, of the bad habits they are acquiring. It will then be difficult to make the right corrections.

FORGET RIGID STANDARDS

Training your voice does not in any way mean matching up to a rigid standard, but it does mean aiming to make your voice fall into an average band which is acceptable to the majority of people. There will be many who will disagree where this average band should lie, but certainly few would question that the extremes at either end present barriers which do nothing to help comprehension. A dialect which, by its very insularity becomes almost a different language, must be criticised as much as the 'Sloane' type of pronunciation favoured by the so-called upper classes of our country, the latter affected speaking being as ludicrous as any variation could be. You will never be able to speak with conviction if the listener pays more attention to the sounds you make than to the message you are trying to convey.

It is perhaps surprising that within Britain, and indeed within the English speaking world, there should be so many variations of the same spoken word and it would certainly be an arrogant assumption that any one of them was the more correct. These variations or dialects are part of our heritage and whether we love them or loathe them, they are with us and need to be accepted as a part of life. Where dialects, or any other variations, become undesirable is when they contribute to being misunderstood, and, for that reason alone, is when any variations need to be corrected. It could be argued that if you never move from the locality in which you were born, this is inconsequential since your own phraseology will be similar to that of your audience. However it will make hard work for yourself and your listeners if you plan to speak, in business or socially, outside that area.

PRESENTATION MATTERS MOST

While it may be in some ways more logical to look first at the vocabulary that we have at our disposal, I believe that we should initially examine the *way* we speak rather than the words we use. Articulation is probably the most difficult discipline in any presentation since it demands that we discard the casual way of speaking that we have been used to most of our lives and insists that we enunciate more clearly so that the listener needs less effort to concentrate. If a speaker already feels that he is readily understood, he will be unwilling to make any change in his style, even if he agrees it will strengthen his message. However, clear enunciation is difficult to acquire since if it is overdone it sounds forced and contrived. Handled correctly it makes for relaxed listening.

The television newscasters who present a skilfully paraphrased description of events are just about the best example of people in the public eye who give top priority to the rule of ensuring that every word and every syllable are both clearly spoken and fully heard. This they achieve in a situation where they are talking to a wide and varied audience with different capacities to absorb what is being said. In general conversation we tend to slur our words, and our words are not chosen so carefully, although the general sense is probably understood. However, in a more formal situation such as selling or public speaking, or even newscasting, words *should* have more importance and consequently their omission or their failure to be heard becomes more critical.

There are methods of speaking in an articulate way, most of which are based on the proper use of the lips and mouth so that the word comes out much like the way it is written. Imagine that your listener is deaf, and relies on lip reading to secure your meaning. When you speak with that picture in mind, your words will immediately sound crisper and properly presented. Overdo that emphasis and you will sound stilted. Your style needs to fit into a pattern somewhere between these two extremes. Casual and careless speech may not be important if you have nothing worthwhile to say but if you wish to convince those to whom you are talking, it is essential to use as many effective tools as you have available.

ENUNCIATE!

Enunciation means that each word we use is an entity in itself. If you become careless and link it up phonetically to the next word (or the one before), it becomes easier to omit the final consonant which gives each word its meaning. The word 'BUT', said on its own, is difficult to vary. However, followed by the word, say, 'YOU', the two words combined swiftly become 'BUTTU' and have already begun to lose their impact.

Words have a beginning and an end, and if in your speaking you are losing one or the other, you are already making it difficult for your listeners to understand what you are saying, and even more so if their ability to follow and interpret is possibly slower than your own. Remember that while many European languages such as Italian or Spanish rely on their vowels for the beauty and style of their presentation, English demands that the consonants are given the most meaning and must be emphasised if you are to convey both clarity and authority. This means projecting what you say and using your lips, not in an exaggerated way, but certainly in a style so that a deaf listener could read your lips and actually be able to understand what you are saying. Bad speakers hardly move their lips at all when they are speaking. Since probably only 60 per cent of their words are actually being heard, this means they are throwing away one of their best chances of being convincing and persuasive. A few rules to ensure your listeners actually hear what you say, are worth listing so that the most common mistakes can be recognised and avoided.

Listen to the clarity of your words

Do you separate your words? Each word has, after all, a meaning of its own, and that meaning is diminished if you combine a word with the preceding or following one, or indeed are careless about pronouncing it at all. Try the last two words and check the difference between 'a tall' and 'at all': the former is the pronunciation that you will most regularly hear. 'Not in', spoken casually, emerges as 'norrin'. Cilla Black has a lot to answer for with 'lorra' instead of 'lot of'. It may be amusing but it *is* slovenly and shows little regard for the listener who has to work hard to understand what has been said.

Listen also to the presenters of quiz shows, or even worse, the teenage presenters of children's television programmes, and you will swiftly see how slovenly use of language (and this to a very young audience) makes what is being said almost unintelligible. The reference to newscasters might well make you think that BBC English is the only criterion to use in judging others. You would be wrong: that thinking was certainly once the situation but times change and we have only to listen to a news broadcast of 40 years ago to realise how stilted it sounds. The aim at that time was to make all speakers sound similar and standardised into a recognizable pattern. Since that time variations in style and presentation have become far more acceptable but the essential rules remain the same. Speech should be easy to absorb, should be interesting both in its vocabulary and its presentation, and should be persuasive in its tone so that it achieves what it is trying to do. That is why dialects (in moderation) are now acceptable while the casual and lazy use of English is not.

Speak more slowly

The 'Del Boy' market approach is one often used by those who believe that a continuous flow of speech is more important than the content. Certainly people will listen, since they are being given little alternative, but they will avoid coming back for more. If you aim for sincerity in your presentation, others will recognise that quality and be prepared to listen. But your own brain, since you know what you are going to say, can easily overtake that of the listener who does not know what he is going to hear. Go at *his* pace, not yours.

Always watch your speed since excessive pace is probably responsible for more bad speaking than anything else. Pace is the speed at which we speak. Not the overall momentum, i.e. a seven minute talk given in five minutes, but the speed which gives importance to one part and less importance to the next. A slow presentation gives emphasis simply because the listener has more time to gather his thoughts and concentrate on what is being said. Generally most people speak too fast, both for their own thoughts and also for their audience to absorb what they are saying. There should, of course, be variation in the speed of presentation of anything that you say, but to emphasise the importance of a particular part of your message, it is essential that your pace slows down to a level which reflects that importance. Listen, if you can, to recorded speeches by Winston Churchill, a man who *always* enunciated every word he uttered, or indeed take note of speakers in the House of Commons, and you will generally be listening to many people who *do* speak well, clearly and slowly, even though they have only limited time available to get their message across. To improve your own standards of volume, tone and pitch, listen all the time to other speakers and endeavour to eliminate in your own voice the peculiarities that you find irritating in others, and adopt those characteristics that others use effectively.

Lower your tone to gain authority

Endeavour to cultivate a deep, rich-sounding voice. Generally your voice will gain by being lowered in tone, and by producing it from the mouth rather than from the nose, you will eliminate the nasal sound which sounds high and forced and contributes nothing to a persuasive image. Rarely will the conviction in your voice be improved by raising the overall tone.

Slower speed in your speech will facilitate a lowering of the pitch of your voice. Pitch has little to do with volume, but can be likened to the variations that you hear in an orchestra. Harsh and even discordant notes in a musical composition can be effective to emphasise a particular passage, but if all the piece is played in that manner, the audience would find it unacceptable. Pitch in your voice can be used to indicate emotion, excitement, even fear, but it is certainly also true that an excessively high, or low, pitch will sometimes convey an emotion which the speaker never intended.

None of us will have to carry our minds too far back to remember a politician of some note who was criticised for being too strident (and so overbearing) and will remember also how that same politician secured a more reasoned voice by lowering her speaking tone. There is no doubt that vocal pitch demands constant attention to avoid it reverting to its original sound since the voice always tends to rise with excitement. However, we should remember that a lower pitched voice is always easier to listen to and excitement and enthusiasm can always be shown in a different way. Children have no such skills at their disposal and I probably do not have to remind you of the irritation caused by a child's tendency to increase pitch to show excitement (or fury)! As an adult speaker we have other means at our disposal: we merely have to learn them.

Monotonous speech is unpersuasive speech

Endeavour to vary your presentation by varying the levels at which you speak. Do not, however, confuse pitch, which is the general tone level of your speech, with inflexion which is the use of a slight variation to emphasise a particular point in your speech. The monotone speaker, at whatever pitch, will sound boring simply because he or she does not vary the intonation. There is no lowering of tone at the end of a sentence nor the raising of tone when a question is being asked.

If you like, the pitch is the tonal effect of what we say. It is the quality which makes a question by using high notes and indicates importance by using low notes. Without it any voice is tedious. With it there is interest and vitality, whether or not the content is of value, but be sure that the variety in projection is only put there by your own emotion and sincerity. If you fail to achieve that sincerity, you also fail in the development in your voice which shows it.

Always regard tone as the warmth you are able to insert into your speaking. Even when listening to people speaking in an unfamiliar foreign language, a great deal can be understood from their inflexion and the way they alter that to make a point. When you listen to people whose words you *do* understand, you gain equally from being able to interpret their manner and their meaning from their presentation as much as from their words. What we say is totally coloured by how we vary that pitch or tone.

Rhythm is also vital, and while it is the quality which distinguishes poetry from prose, it is also the quality which distinguishes good conversation from bad. Some people have natural rhythm and are pleasant to listen to whatever their subject, while in others (the majority), the quality has to be cultivated. How we speak and the way in which we balance phrases together to give a style to the whole is probably most noticeable in poetry where a formal rhythm is used to give the right emphasis. In speaking also we need to cultivate the same kind of rhythm to give a pleasantly acceptable format to our speech. Long sentences, whether in speech or in writing, are confusing to the listener who finds himself unable to sort out the important parts from those less important. A shorter style tends to outline more clearly the points that the speaker (or the writer) is aiming to make and enables the speaker also to vary his pitch (and tone) within the sentence. In this way he can give the right inflexion and importance to the points he is trying to get across.

Don't forget to pause!

Be conscious of the necessity of breaking your conversation with pauses. These are as much value to you as they are to the listener. The times when you do *not* speak help you to:

- prepare for your next thought or idea;
- give a further rhythm to what you are saying; and
- guide your listener to be prepared for a change of angle or indeed a change of topic.

Think of a pause as similar to a paragraph in your writing. Without it, your voice would sound as dull and uninteresting as a book with no paragraphs at all. The pause will also be valuable to you in controlling the pace at which you make your own presentation. Again, listen to the speeches of Winston Churchill and recognise how he uses those pauses (and long pauses at that) to lead into the most important content of his speeches. 'Never (*pause*) in the field of human conflict (*pause*) has so much (*pause*) been owed by so many (*pause*) to so few.' Probably his best-known quotation, but one where the use of pauses is no more or less masterly than his daily speeches in the House of Commons. Conversation is no different to public speaking in that those pauses provide the conviction that a rushed presentation does not.

The pause should be considered as a deliberate stop in the flow of speech and is designed to:

■ secure attention from those whose minds might be wandering;

■ hold that interest and make the listener anticipate what might be coming next;

■ stimulate interest in what *has* been said, giving, if you like, a brief review so that particular point is logged in memory.

Pause and give silences more frequently than you believe to be necessary. A dramatic pause in any conversational situation will hold your audience's attention while they wait for your next words. Listen to any good theatre production and recognise how much time is taken up by nothing being said at all. Silence is a vital tool in speech.

Benefit from controlled breathing

Be aware that good breathing is a key to good speaking. Most good articulation and rhythm relies on it since it is from good breathing that the tonal quality of your voice really comes. Rarely is a nasal sound attractive, yet by shifting the source of it from your nose to your chest, you can lower the tone of your voice at the same time. Leaving aside the fact that this will make your voice easier to hear, it will also sound more pleasant and easier for you to vary the tone of the presentation. Many actors and politicians have proved that it *is* possible to create a different voice for themselves which grates less with their audience. The mouth and tongue will always shape the final twang or sharpness to words but the basic timbre of the voice will come from the chest and the lungs.

Your volume must suit your listener

Plan the volume that you need to suit your environment and your listeners, and never use volume to force a point of view. Volume is simply the way we use loudness to make a point. A quiet phrase can often give the same importance, but variation is certainly necessary to emphasise the change from one priority to the next. Again to use Winston Churchill as an example, he rarely shouted, but you will find that his volume control was used constantly to indicate to his listener whether he was giving emphasis or not. Assuming your voice is normal, you should never need to shout to make yourself heard. Certainly your diaphragm may have to work harder – that is what it is for – but that should be the only adjustment needed to compensate for a large room or difficult surroundings.

The overall control of volume is of course important since many people simply do not speak clearly or loud enough to be understood at all. If the group you are talking to is large (whether or not the room is small), always speak beyond the person who is furthest away from you. That means articulating more clearly so that every word of what you *do* say reaches its destination. Change of volume or power will emphasise a word, particularly if it follows a pause. Decreasing your volume, or even worse, losing the stress at the end of a sentence, is rarely effective unless you can be sure that the audience can still hear you. If they cannot, as is probably the case, then you will have lost the impact of what you wanted to say. Listen to any general conversation in a pub or wherever and you can see how 40 per cent of words that are spoken are either not heard or misunderstood. You will hear unfinished sentences, often unplanned and unstructured – therefore unmeaningful.

DIALECT

Previously I have mentioned briefly the subject of dialect. Contrary to some opinions, it would be foolish to believe that there is *not* prejudice against dialect in areas geographically away from its home county. Certainly dialect, particularly in children, is often attractive and our country would be less rich without it, but for all that it brings disadvantages of which the speaker or salesman should be aware. The main problem is that dialect represents a style and character which is only used in one part of the country and may well be incomprehensible elsewhere. In some cases a dialect may need to be modified to ensure that it does not detract from the audience's comprehension. Recently there has been great emphasis on encouraging local dialects in the belief that they are a part of our heritage and should, at all costs, be protected for future generations. An understandable principle, but if you are aiming to be universal in your speaking so that you speak effectively and persuasively wherever you go, then you also need to be understood wherever you go. The simple rule is that for pronunciation to be correct, it must be acceptable to the listener and I would question whether some of the heavier dialects we now hear in TV dramas, for example, do anything but infuriate those who have to concentrate hard on what is actually being said. Strong dialects are rarely a good means of communication, and they are *not* as desirable as many 'free-thin-kers' would have you believe.

CORRECT YOUR GRAMMAR

We must briefly consider grammar, although I say briefly somewhat reluctantly. There is little time in a book of this nature to analyse the requirements of grammar to ensure that you are taken seriously and that you use words and phrases which are correct. Correct grammar is essential for anyone aiming to sound convincing, and if your grammar is poor, then you may have to live with it, but you will certainly have to improve in other directions to make up for the disadvantages. Poor grammar will divert the listener's attention from *what* you are saying to *how* you are saying it. In social conversation it will jar in the same way and affect the way you are regarded. There is no kinder way of stating what is a simple fact.

Simple errors such as 'I were just going into town', 'You was getting in my way', 'He done that', 'He never told me nothing' or 'I ain't coming with you' are fine for the TV soaps, and may seem so common that you might think they have no effect on the listener, but such errors will have a damaging effect on your reputation. In addition, if you are aware of the problem but cannot correct it, then it destroys any confidence in your own ability to move in circles more educated than your own. Forcing yourself into the right patterns of grammar involves, first, recognition of the errors and secondly, hard work to change what is probably a lifetime of doing it the wrong way. Not easy but little that is worthwhile is easy.

Believe me, poor grammar, inarticulate speaking and confused sentences can ruin any good conversation or speech as much as the lack of intelligent content and it is only the inarticulate speaker who will claim that content is all that matters. Articulation is many skills but a great number of them come back to seeing each vowel, seeing each consonant, and pronouncing words so that each vowel and consonant is actually there. Then the final result is smoothed to avoid the stilted effect of over-pronunciation. This vital exercise will ensure that people hear every word you are saying rather than every third or fourth word. Speaking clearly and using each word carefully will initially need conscious practice, but it is probably the easiest adjustment of all to make to your presentation and is certainly a foundation on which all other improvements in your speech should be based.

Finally, make use of a tape recorder to monitor your progress regularly and check whether you have unwelcome characteristics of presentation which you recognise in others. A tape recorder gives you the only real impression of what you actually sound like to others. If you don't believe me, try covering your ears and then speak. You will still hear yourself – but nothing else – indicating how much of the impression of your own voice comes from inside and how little of it really compares with what others hear when they listen to you. Find an honest friend to act as an independent arbiter of your progress.

CHECKLIST

- Sticking to set standards of grammar is not necessary.
- Listen and learn from the style of the professionals.
- Keep it clear – separate each word from the next.
- Watch your speed – and don't forget the pauses.
- Insert variety by altering the tone and volume of what you say.
- If your grammar grates, you have lost your listener.
- Listen to yourself as others hear you – and make improvements.

3

Ways with words

'Remember,' said Pooh, 'that I am a BEAR OF VERY LITTLE BRAIN, and long words bother me'.

Chapter Four, *Winnie The Pooh*, A A Milne (1882–1956)

The English language consists of some 700,000 words, and while it would be foolish to think we could have all of these at our disposal, the limited number of words that the majority of people actually do use (probably around 3000–5000) is an indictment of a teaching system that permits students to get away with the minimum vocabulary necessary to be understood. Fortunately you *can* increase your vocabulary making your speech more colourful and convincing, and increasing your own self-confidence in being able to say the right thing at the right time.

While the way we produce our words must remain one of the most important aspects of our style and technique, the actual words we have at our disposal and the correct use of them will always mark the good speaker from the bad and the amateur from the professional. A limited vocabulary indicates complacency; someone who has not taken the trouble to absorb into his own usage the words he hears from others every day.

INCREASING YOUR VOCABULARY IS EASY

Although the words we use form only a part of what we say, because our skill with them is probably the easiest to improve it is worth spending some time to ensure that we have the widest choice available to us. In addition, if we do *not* have words easily available to us, that tends to reduce our ability to convey the sincerity and enthusiasm which, for any good speaker, is essential.

In choosing words, there is one danger which must be avoided, and that is making the creation of language, whether spoken or written, such an intellectual exercise that it tries to force everyone down the same narrow channel. Even now an attempt is being made, in the form of computer-designed grammar checks, to reject any variation from the norm. This is not what selection of words is about but it *is* about sounding correct and not sounding contrived. Some of the best writers in the world took liberties both with the use of grammar and the choice of words and made their writing more alive and readable because of it.

Similarly, you need to beware of those who tell you that there is only one way to pronounce a word. Words such as controversy, dispute, kilometre, research and many others vary in their pronunciation. My own belief is that in private conversation, so long as there are two (or even three) well accepted alternatives, then this matters little. However, if you are speaking to a wider audience, it is probably advisable to opt for the most commonly heard pronunciation, or if possible, the one which is most familiar to your listeners.

ELIMINATING CONFUSION

Many words are incorrectly applied, for example practice and practise, complimentary and complementary, insure and ensure. There is really only one way to get these right and that is to make note of them every time you read them elsewhere. If you have any doubt, use a dictionary. There are few words anyway in this category and once you have them correctly labelled, you will probably have little difficulty again.

Although increasing one's vocabulary is relatively easy it does, like all other skills, demand a discipline to recognise the words that are worth adding to one's repertoire, and to make the effort to use them until they come automatically to mind. To help in this, the importance of reading to develop one's word power cannot be overemphasised. If you fail to read, whether it be newspapers, magazines or books, and merely skim through the content as most people do, you will have the same vocabulary at the end of your life as at the beginning, and moreover will probably not understand half of what you *have* skimmed through. You cannot make your own speech more interesting without consciously borrowing from others, but you should always remember that an extensive vocabulary, however valuable, can also confuse those whose vocabularies do not match up to your own.

DEVELOP YOUR EXISTING VOCABULARY

Many speakers who admit to having problems will tell you that they are rarely short of ideas but often have difficulty in finding the right words to express them. My belief is that they simply do not go deep enough into their minds to find the right words. More than likely they will know the word they want to use, but because they have not thought out the meaning when they first saw it, they have not stored it away for a particular application in the future. The immediate availability of words is something which probably causes more nervousness and fear of speaking, both socially and publicly, than any other, since it inevitably slows down your conversation to a level where you may well be groping for the next word you require. A good speaker will *always* have available far more words than he is likely to use.

The acquisition and use of a better vocabulary is time consuming but otherwise relatively easy. It does not demand reading a dictionary and adding words with which you are not familiar to your own list. Certainly, the use of a dictionary or thesaurus will enable you to clarify a word's meaning, but what an expanded vocabulary *does* demand is the constant reading of other people's literature and recognising appropriate words which suit your own style, and which can be transferred to your own speaking or written style. That is the way that College and University English is studied – and why not, when there are so many other examples available which you can lift or adapt to your own presentation. I cannot overemphasise the importance of increasing your vocabulary if you wish to improve your own speaking style. A regular feature of *Reader's Digest* is a feature called 'It pays to increase your word power': regular checking through this feature or a similar one is a guaranteed way of finding colourful words which you might not have considered until now.

Although some words may well have the same meaning as others, some sound better than others and the following rules will help you to choose those words.

Aim for simplicity

Don't use complicated words believing them necessarily to be more impressive. This is particularly important where the meaning of the complicated word might not readily be understood by your audience. For example, we all have to think hard when a word such as 'ambivalence' is used, whereas in most cases the word 'indecision' will say the same thing. Why make it difficult for the listener to understand when making him understand is the sole object of your speaking? By all means use less obvious words from time to time, but only if you are totally confident as to their meaning, and you are also confident that they are within the understanding of your audience. Experimenting with tortuous words often fails to get the message through to the listener, particularly to those who have a limited capacity to understand.

Shorter words are more effective

Even when the word, or phrase, is understood, try to keep the meaning simple by using a shorter, more concise word, or even one word in place of two. 'Multitude of' rarely means other than many, but some people will use any word rather than the simple positive ones. Supercalifragelistic etc is *not* clever speaking although Mary Poppins (and many others) would have you believe that the longer the words you use, the higher your intelligence. Don't fall into the same trap. 'At this moment of time' means 'now'. 'As an immediate result of your action' means 'because you did'. 'Endeavour to achieve' usually means 'try'. All the second choices are not only easier to write than the first but they are also stronger and give more impact to your views.

Certainly the use of expansive and decorated words is a habit of many verbose people, and by doing so in circumstances which are unnecessary, those people lose the ability to use them where they *would* have impact. Keep your superlative words for superlative situations and they will then have the effect your desire. Even the casual use of 'thank you very much indeed' (instead of 'thank you') is a typical case of overstatement.

Choose words with impact

In choosing your words, always aim to use words which have impact. That does not mean words which startle your listener by appearing out of place but it does mean words which express more clearly and forcefully than the mundane ones what you are trying to say. The choice of good words that fit that pattern is rarely made if you do not have a wide selection to work from in the first place. Again, reading will tell you which words impress you and which words should be added to your own vocabulary. If you have a small vocabulary, you will become repetitive and so lose the impact of the words you do have available.

While keeping your vocabulary as simple as possible, aim to have a wide range available, using words other than the everyday ones which people would expect you to use. This means finding a proper balance between the prosaic, everyday words and the overconfusing, longer words.

Pictorial and descriptive words give maximum effect

Aim to use colourful and descriptive words which paint an imaginative picture rather than those which the listener will have to picture for himself. 'White clouds' says one thing. 'Fluffy white clouds' says something far more effective. A speaker who creates images saves the audience the work of doing it for themselves, or indeed, if they have low interest in what is being said, not doing it at all. Compare the description, 'It was a large cupboard' with (far better) 'It was a cavernous cupboard'; one a base adjective, one a pictorial description. You might well argue that the first choice is shorter, but the second is certainly more vivid. In the words of O Henry, 'Words fluttered from him like swallows leaving a barn at daylight'. Maybe too ambitious an aim for yourself but a move in that direction can only be of advantage.

Eliminate vagueness

Get rid of the 'actually' and 'in facts' of this world. These and similar phrases are meaningless and used in excess will even get your listener focusing on those phrases rather than what you have to say. Other waffle phrases, such as 'you know', 'I mean' and 'well' all indicate that the speaker has no really clear idea of what he wants to say. If he had thought ahead, there would have been no need for such space-fillers which weaken overall meaning. This is a generalisation, however; as with most things, used in moderation, these phrases can be as valuable as any others.

Each word that you use should have a positive reason for being there and while the aim to achieve that is probably overoptimistic, it will nevertheless make you constantly aware of the need to eliminate the words and phrases which have no reason to be there at all.

Avoid jargon

Try not to use ambiguous words or unfamiliar terms. It is only the empathy of the speaker that can decide what words will be understood by those listening and even when talking socially it is courteous to use familiar words rather than unfamiliar ones. An enthusiastic golfer, describing his day's play, might well be understood by half his audience when he talks of sandirons and slicing, but he is certain to bore the other half with language which is unfamiliar to them. If he *wants* to entertain that other 50 per cent, he must modify, or explain, some of the words he is saying so that he appeals to as wide an audience as possible.

In the same rule, avoid the words which technical people use to each other. Even if 90 per cent of your listeners understand, it is discourteous to the other 10 per cent. Doctors insist on using convoluted words to describe a simple headache. Landscape gardeners use technical Latin words to describe a simple conifer. Politicians and economists use phrases and sentences which no-one understands at all. Even at the risk of using words which some might find too simple, choose words which all your audience will understand.

Emphasise your words carefully

Finally, look closely at the accent that you place on each word. Words necessarily need emphasis in different ways and the meaning of a simple phrase can be changed by placing your stress on different words. For example, in the sentence 'I am taking the car today', the meaning differs depending on which word is emphasised and the phraseology in a simple sentence like this indicates how much you can change meaning or convey a different impression simply by inflexion rather than a change of the actual words:

I am taking our car.
I *am* taking our car.
I am *taking* our car.
I am taking *our* car.
I am taking our *car*.

The development of your vocabulary is a continuing process of analysing those occasions when you do not have available the words that you need and always reading with the conscious effort of absorbing the words of others. If you wish, use a thesaurus to select a more appropriate alternative. The ability to produce, either orally or verbally, what might be described as colourful language (in the true sense), is a satisfying art to have at your command and it is often neglected because speakers, and writers, do not recognise their own limited vocabulary nor improve on it. It is only part of good communication but it is a large enough part to warrant your close attention.

The use of all words is simply to convey an image which can be clearly understood by the listener. You have in your own mind a picture of what you are trying to say; you choose a word which should represent that picture and it is then converted back into an image which the listener recognises. If that is not the same image in the minds of both speaker and listener, your communication has failed: you have chosen the wrong word to communicate with that particular person. Consider a listener who speaks little English and you will immediately be aware that if you use complicated words (even said in a loud voice) he will not understand what message you are trying to convey. You need to adjust your own vocabulary to suit a listener with a limited knowledge of words at his disposal. This rule applies in any situation: the choice of words must be related to the recipient. Remember that words are essential tools to communicate and get your message across – you may as well aim to choose the best words that will do just that.

CHECKLIST

- Increase your vocabulary by reading more.
- Use simple pictorial words to convey images.
- Eliminate indecisive words.
- Use only words to which your listener can relate.
- Develop your vocabulary continuously.

4

Preparing your ideas in a logical way

He is one of those orators of whom it was said. Before they get up they do not know what they are going to say; when they are speaking they do not know what they are saying; and when they sit down they do not know what they have said.

Winston Churchill speaking of Lord Charles Beresford in the House of Commons on 12 December 1912

There are, of course, professional speakers who have the ability and skill to make a success of virtually any topic of conversation they choose. This usually is only achieved with a great deal of preparation, although there are people who speak naturally well and have a gift for speaking 'off the cuff'. Unfortunately the majority of us are not like that; we need to prepare for what we are planning to say. For social and general conversation this is basically a simple matter of being well read so that we have at our disposal a vast range of information to drawn on, enabling us to illustrate what we are saying with practical detail and quotations relevant to the topic. Any back-up like this is essential to making our own conversation convincing and knowledgeable.

For a more formal speech, privately or in business, we need to be not only well read but we also need to plan logically so that we not only use the information we have researched, but use it in as logical and effective a way as possible. A speech or a business presentation must, like a book, have structure: a proper start, a proper ending, and adequate filling in the middle to satisfy the reader (or listener). Good planning is the only way for most of us to achieve this discipline. It is the height of amateurism to apologise beforehand for lack of preparation – the listener will make up his own mind anyway and an apology in advance will give him all the reasons he needs to reject what you are saying. If you need to make such an apology, you should not be speaking in the first place.

PREPARATION IS VITAL

One of the main reasons why many people cannot convey their thoughts is that they rarely pause to consider what they are going to say, and indeed who they are going to say it to, before they actually speak. *Always* in speaking, whether it be a selling presentation, a lecture, or simply an everyday conversation, you must have a definite format which is well thought out, practical to use, and one which you know beforehand will be acceptable to those who have to listen to it. Remember that if you are apprehensive because of a lack of content, or think you will antagonise your audience rather than convince them, this will lead you into grammatical and phrasing errors and take away from the self-confidence you have carefully nurtured. The more you are aware that you have planned and prepared against most of the eventualities which might arise, the less you will be conscious of the risk of that happening. Remember that you are being constantly judged by your friends, by your employer, by your customers and by your general listeners. If those others recognise your own self-confidence then you have a far greater chance of being accepted by them as someone with something worthwhile to say.

Although this chapter is directed chiefly towards formal, rather than general, conversation, a great deal of it is relevant to the way you put your thoughts together *at any time*. Do not disregard the rules simply because you rarely speak in public. For the purpose of this chapter, let us assume that you need to prepare a formal talk or sales presentation and, with that in mind, you are looking for the most practical framework on which to build.

GETTING THE FRAMEWORK RIGHT

In considering any format, a skeleton of your presentation or ideas must be made first. The introduction should probably take up around 10 per cent of the total speech, should summarise the theme of your talk, and list in a logical order the points you plan to make. It is, after all, not unreasonable to spend three minutes outlining what you are going to say for the next thirty, and such an introduction should allow time for you to give your own qualifications for speaking at all so that your audience has time to prejudge your own capabilities.

Your opening, whatever you choose to say, should be pertinent, relevant, and touched with, if not humour, at least humanity. People want to relate to something personal and while statistics or facts may be important later on, be wary of inserting them into your opening sentence. By all means, if they are dramatic facts, use them to awake interest (and the audience). At the opening of any talk, sales presentation, or indeed conversation, your listeners are looking hard for an indication that what you have to say will be worth more of their attention. A few minutes later is probably too late to convey that impression. Equally important is your choice of ending since *that* is what you will be remembered for. Making all your important points at the beginning and then being forced to fade at the end is a guaranteed way of ensuring that the first part of what you have said is totally overshadowed by the last. A strong ending is important particularly if you are making a formal presentation, and when planning you should make use of the fact that your audience will give your final words more attention than the rest. Remember that a good magician always keeps his best trick to the end. You would be well advised to do the same.

While on the subject of the programme, remember that in any situation where you are working to a schedule, *time is vital*. You must keep to the plan you have made and, if you must deviate, it must only be to make it shorter. It is always far better to leave your audience wanting (or even asking) for more than to have them showing you that you have gone on for too long.

If your subject involves imparting information, your framework should fall into four clear sections:

1. Introduction (eg to your own research into a business topic);

2. Justification for the work being done at all;

3. Outlining the results of the research that has been undertaken;

4. Conclusions

Into each of these sections, the key points can then be highlighted in your notes as an *aide-memoire* when you are speaking. Illogically you will often find it simpler to write this format in reverse, starting with the last part, since all you are going to say will be leading to the final conclusion.

A framework is essential in any talk and it relies on repeating the main points and integrating them into the remainder of what you are saying. All listeners have different demands and if they know that their particular approach is the same as yours, they will concentrate on those parts where you are emphasising that approach and be prepared to tolerate the intermediate stages which might not interest them as much. If you wander from topic to topic without an obvious framework, you will lose their attention altogether. Regular repetition of that framework will help in carrying with you those whose ability to concentrate might not be as well developed as your own.

KNOW WHAT YOUR AUDIENCE WANTS

All really effective speaking results from a study of those who are going to listen to you. Is your audience receptive or possibly even hostile? There *are* hostile audiences, particularly in the political or local authority arenas where you may find yourself putting forward an unwelcome proposition to a group whose views are totally opposed to your own. A speech or a talk on the closing of a local hospital needs somewhat more careful handling than a speech proposing the opening of a new one.

The analysis of your audience has a great bearing on how you express what you are trying to put across and what reaction you expect from them. What is the object of your speaking – are you aiming to convince, to sell, to inform, or even just entertain? Your empathy in analysing their wants is vital if at the end of your speech you expect your audience to react by being happy with what you have said. This applies whether you are talking to one person or a hundred. The Rugby Club will be looking for one sort of speaker, the Mother's Union another. Fail to recognise that difference and you will probably upset both. Similarly the business person who refuses to tailor his conversation to the person it is aimed at need not be surprised when it does not have the impact it should.

There will also be a difference in the reason why your audience is there. Are they there voluntarily or compulsorily? If the former, they will be more prepared to reach out to you. If the latter, they may well have put up a barrier before you start. The variation in your presentation and the plan for it will need to be different to match each set of circumstances.

If you are speaking in a business presentation or a more informal occasion, you will need to know beforehand how informed is your audience. If you are an amateur computer buff and you are talking to experts, you will have little hope, however good a conversationalist you are, of holding your audience. If it is a social conversation, beware of making a fool of yourself among those who will recognise your limitations. Better to become knowledgeable in some other topic and have a view which might be listened to, than take the risk of being ignored simply because you have no well-informed view to give.

FOLLOW A LOGICAL PLAN

Later on in this book, and dealing specifically with talking to wider audiences, I shall be covering the preparation of what you are going to say and how to put your ideas together so that one follows logically from the next. That is probably the hardest part of any planning, but a few suggestions in this chapter will be useful in guiding your thinking.

Get your thoughts down on paper: When you are preparing a talk or a presentation, always write down your ideas as they occur. Call it brainstorming if you like, but long before you arrange those thoughts in a logical way, make sure that you have them written down (or even recorded on tape) as you think of them. It is far more difficult to assemble thoughts if you try to place them in order before you have made a note of what they are. Rearranging them can come later when you have prepared the framework into which they will go.

Have an object in view before you start: To make your presentation more persuasive and assertive, know beforehand exactly what you want to say. This does not necessarily mean the words you are going to say since the detail can come later, but it means a clear picture of the result you are looking for. It also means planning your content so that your listener equally recognises that objective.

Give prior importance to the beginning and the end: Spend as much time on your first 10 per cent and the last 10 per cent of your talk as you spend on the remaining 80 per cent. You will be judged totally out of proportion to the amount of time you spend on each. A good starting point is vital to take advantage of the high point in the concentration of your listener.

Use humour and joke-telling skilfully: By all means use humour, but remember that does not necessarily mean telling jokes. It certainly *never* means telling irrelevant jokes, and, unless you are a professional comedian, it certainly does not mean using them in that valuable start and finish time, when you have the keenest attention from your audience anyway. Particularly at the beginning, after any laughter has subsided you are then forced to bring the listener back to the real topic of your talk. Do not make the mistake of believing that laughter as a response is necessarily an indication of success. There are few good raconteurs and fewer original stories and it is as well to remember the words of Irvin S Cobb who said, 'A good storyteller is a person who has a good memory and hopes other people haven't'.

Avoid unplanned speeches: Finally, when considering planning remember that there should *never* be impromptu speeches – only speeches which listeners think are impromptu. All speeches should be prepared with equal thoroughness. There are few speakers who are really capable of a genuine impromptu speech and, even if they are, that speech can always be improved by additional preparation beforehand.

If you are speaking impromptu because of inadequate preparation time, remember that all impromptu speaking demands an unusual ability to plan, to be logical, to be understood, all skills taking place at the same time while you are standing in front of your audience. Good impromptu speakers probably *do* exist, but certainly they do not include the majority of the greatest speakers of our time, all of whom believed in extensive planning and preparation before even considering getting to their feet. Even Winston Churchill described the preparation of a speech as one of the hardest jobs he had to do, and except in the earliest part of his life, would *never* speak impromptu. A preplanned framework is always essential so that you have something on which to build the rest.

With a logical plan, whatever the occasion, you will also achieve added self-confidence, knowing that the direction you are taking is the one you have anticipated and rehearsed, and that, all being well, there will be no unexpected surprises along the way. The art of any good speaker is to eliminate as many of the gremlins as possible and, in conjunction with the choice of words and the style of presentation, the plan that you actually work to is of equally high importance. Remember that nervousness is generally the fear of the unexpected and the greater your anticipation of what might happen, the higher the level of your own confidence that you can handle it should it occur.

CHECKLIST

■ Plan what you have to say as logically as you can.

■ Be aware of what your listeners expect you to say.

■ Don't use humour in the wrong context.

■ Avoid unprepared and impromptu presentations.

■ Eliminate the unexpected so that you develop your self-confidence.

5

The rules of general conversation

When you were quite a little boy, somebody ought to have said 'hush' just once.

Letter to George Bernard Shaw, November 1912

Why, in a book on presentation or speaking, is there a chapter on general conversation? Simply because, in your job as a business professional, that is the area in which you are projecting yourself, and whether your listener is the bank manager, the audience at a Round Table function, a Rotary Club Dinner, or a family wedding, you need to come across as a person who is confident of his ability in whatever other aspect of the job you are trying to promote. We must all live and breathe in many other environments outside our own business circles and your job will be far easier if you have learnt how to handle conversation in your everyday life.

The reasons why speakers and their listeners get it right or wrong in public speaking are identical to the reasons why people succeed or fail in their general conversation. People who are hesitant to speak, even in a room full of people they already know, will usually give the same reasons every time for being hesitant.

■ 'I have no difficulty in *knowing* what I want to say, but I do have difficulty in getting my thoughts into a logical plan so that I can express them.'

■ 'I have little self-confidence in my ability to hold the interest of others.'

- 'I have no general knowledge of topics arising in everyday discussion, so am unable to talk beyond a few obvious facts which I feel sure everyone else knows already.'

- 'I am aware of the limitations of my vocabulary and my grammar and believe that my listeners will constantly be on the watch for words that I misuse.'

SELF-CONFIDENCE IS THE KEY

Most of the reasons listed above stem from a lack of basic confidence, something which can be eliminated by, first, developing (through reading and listening) a wider knowledge of at least *one* topic where you have some information you can confidently transmit to others, and secondly, by working on your vocabulary by listening to others whose interpretation of grammar and usage is probably reliable (newscasters are as good an example as any), and then adding words to your vocabulary which appear to have more conviction than those you use already. The solutions lie in making yourself aware of more colourful language and being prepared to absorb what you hear so that you can make use of it yourself later.

In all matters of expressing ourselves, once we have decided the words we plan to use, a great deal still rests on how we put our phrases together and how we convince, not only our listener, but more essentially, ourselves, that we have enthusiasm and conviction about our topic; positive thinking and positive talking. This is the difference between someone who says they will '*try* to phone you next Wednesday' and the person who says 'I *will* telephone you next Wednesday'. There is probably no great difference in what you are actually meaning to convey but there is every difference in the way the two statements are received by the listener; the difference between a vague intention and a definite plan. If you always speak powerfully and positively and aim to avoid the negatives which apologise before you actually say anything, you will raise your own level of assurance and raise it also in the opinion of your listener.

There *are* people who cannot enter a room full of strangers without feeling intimidated, believing they have nothing to contribute to the conversation. It is particularly this attitude of mind which increases someone's lack of self-confidence since he convinces himself before he starts that he will fail unless something unexpected happens to stop it.

The real attitude of mind is to become convinced that you *will* succeed unless the unexpected happens. You need to ask yourself whether people actually listen to you when you speak or are they merely waiting for a space to get their own word in? If they are not listening they will not react and if reaction is what you are seeking, you are not communicating effectively at all. Many people have the knowledge to make their point but to not have the ability to talk with conviction. Many people have the opposite. Your aim should be to be competent in both.

SUCCESS IN SOCIAL CIRCLES

If you fail in your business speaking you stand to lose a great deal, possibly even your employment. If you fail in your private life, you merely, and I use the word advisedly, lose your acceptance in the social circles in which you might wish to move. General social conversation is essentially to entertain and to make your audience feel happy at listening to you. In most cases an audience is interested only in one thing: themselves. What is being said, however skilfully, must relate to them and if it does not, their concentration will soon be lost. The average Sunday preacher fails because he does not relate at all; he is merely giving his own personal interpretation of a subject, rather than providing something which his audience wants to hear. The skilful speaker will endeavour to steer a middle course between both objectives.

In a more formal way, this may well consist of complimenting your listeners as an audience, by praising someone who is retiring from business or by wishing a newly married couple best wishes for the future. If you become known as someone who is capable of expressing himself clearly and entertainingly, it is as well to know the guidelines which enable you to do it with more panache than others.

EMPATHY IS VITAL

What any good speaker must do in social conversation is to get inside his audience. Like any other speaking, this does demand making the best use of the skills that, with training, you can acquire. Even speaking to a small social audience needs to conform to a format and discipline. In any conversation there are rules which will give you the ability to hold an audience. Surprisingly the most important, listed below, are not concerned with diction or with style:

Make sure you have knowledge of your subject: Always talk about something which is part of your own experience of life; a subject of which you have personal knowledge. Many speakers talk on subjects where their only knowledge is through hurried research and are then surprised when accused of not knowing their subject. At the very least make sure that what you say is coloured by something which is topical, using references to the recently expressed opinions of others. For instance, if the state of the economy is a must in your repertoire, then ensure you are au fait with experts' predictions, be it a depression in Sicily or a boom in Saratoga. Develop a wide range of topics on which you have valid opinions and you will rarely run short of something to say. Lack of knowledge of a topic is certainly reflected in the way you speak and your tentative assertions. Improve that knowledge and you will find that your voice, and the authority it carries, will improve also.

Be aware that others need time to absorb your opinions: Remember that if you are expressing what, to you, is a long-held opinion, this may still be new to the listener – he may not have your familiarity with the subject. Pause frequently so that others can absorb what you say and can make contributions themselves.

Respect the contrary views of others: Always have a natural respect for opposing views and values, even though you may disagree with them. If you dismiss other opinions out of hand you will gain the reputation of being abrasive. If you *know* that your views will irritate others, you will certainly not secure any agreement and it is better either to modify those views or alternatively not express them at all. An often-quoted piece of advice is 'Those who speak straight from the shoulder should try from a little higher up.' Often it takes only a little thought to make that adjustment.

What one person may see as a discussion, another may see as an argument and in situations like this, the inevitable loss of control by one or the other ensures that an argument is just what it becomes. The conflict can be avoided altogether by climbing down, albeit temporarily, from your own opinions. A typical example is the work of the Foreign Office and the Diplomatic Corps, whose main business is to express an opinion but to keep the doors open for continuing their discussions. In our general conversation, a similar skill is often required to avoid conflict or argument creeping in to what may well have started as a reasoned discussion.

Back up your opinions with personal experience: Aim to look for subjects in your own immediate past where you have something of consequence to say and confine yourself to that approach to the subject. There are many budding Chancellors of the Exchequer in every public house and at every cocktail party but few who ever have the knowledge and experience to relate their observations to some experience in the past which gives them authority to express their opinion. You can always link your opinion with conversations you have had with others you have met and with whom you might have exchanged views on the same subject. Remember those views for later use.

Choose topics which match the interests of your listeners: Ensure that what you do say has a good prospect of being interesting, both in its opening and in the way such a conversation can be developed. In addition it should not have the threat of becoming argumentative. An opening gambit of 'I think boxing is stupid and dangerous' is fine if you know your audience (and possibly if you are a brain surgeon and have first-hand technical knowledge of the subject), but if you do not, you could well be heading for an argument before you have even started. That does not mean that controversial topics are banned but it certainly means that they should not provide the opening of a conversation with someone you have not met before.

Make your approach to a listener personal and special: Aim to talk to your listener as if he or she is the only other person in the room. Aim to listen as if the speaker is all-important. By creating that sort of atmosphere you will achieve a flow of conversation between two people who are receptive to each other. It may well be difficult since many speakers may make it hard for you to be interested in them, but remember that as listeners they might be having the same problem with you.

Choose your opening with care: To avoid killing a conversation before you start, never start any social conversation with a cliché. This means forgetting about the weather and all the other standards. It means avoiding the 'Do you come here often?' approach. If, for instance, you are at a party, the listener may have heard the same remark a dozen times already and it is worthwhile making an effort to ensure that your initial remark is at least original.

Ask questions and listen for the answers: To keep any conversation going, you need to ask questions rather than make statements. If you can, you should also try to relate those questions to the last point that the other person made. This is, after all, the way you will see a quality interviewer working on television, so drawing out a flow of information from someone who might otherwise be too withdrawn to offer it. Good conversation is encouraging someone else to talk, rather than monopolising the conversation yourself. Constantly asking questions will encourage a listener to participate more.

Make the conversation two-way: In the early stages of any conversation, be aware constantly of the need to pass the initiative back to the listener. Hopefully he will do the same. However, if he then monopolises the conversation, it will be a useful reminder of the effect it has on *you* if you have something further to say and are not being given the opportunity to do so. If you monopolise the conversation yourself, do not be surprised if you suddenly find yourself with no-one left to talk to.

Preparation means having something to say: Prepare what you have to say as much as you would a public presentation. A private audience will sometimes accept poor elocution but will not excuse lack of care in preparing the content.

Interest in others, not yourself, is all-important: Your subject must be the others in the room, not you. Make it an ego trip and the audience, who want you to talk about *them*, will show their disinterest. As an example of how it should be done, the best man at a wedding should always talk about the groom, not about himself. The same guidelines should influence your attitude to the demands of others.

Your speed of speaking is crucial: Remember all the previous advice about speaking slowly and with precision, and then slow down yet again. Slow speech is the key to being listened to and appreciated. You are making it easier for your listener and that is a plus point on its own. Use pauses effectively and remember that without them you are creating the same kind of confusion as a paragraph without punctuation, so making it difficult for the listener to identify where the emphasis should be and where one idea stops and where the next one starts.

Your ideas should have impact and value: Whatever you are talking about, aim to avoid generalisation or abstract ideas and plan to be specific. Once you have decided your own limitations and the knowledge of your topic, stay within those limitations. A bad conversationalist who is not specific can be compared to a three-day coach trip of Europe. It can be done but no specific area is properly covered and no real importance is given to any part of it. If you want people to listen to you, you must provide them with something that they, as listeners, can appreciate and acknowledge as an addition to their own knowledge.

Real enthusiasm for your subject will show: Always talk about subjects that you are *really* enthusiastic about. If politics do not greatly interest you, or your general knowledge of them is slim, then your views on the politics (or the politicians) of the day will have no great interest either. Either develop your interest in the topic or change your subject altogether. With a high degree of knowledge, enthusiasm and obvious sincerity, you can almost compel others to listen to your views whether those views have validity or not. The same sort of enthusiasm must equally be shown when you are a listener, and you should *never* show a lack of interest in others by interrupting with your own views. Wait until the buck is passed back to you and then ensure that you do not encourage others to stop you talking.

Build your relationships gradually: Always remember that in your general conversation the over-familiar approach can often alienate those you are trying to impress. Even the immediate use of a Christian name causes offence to some people who prefer to make a point of inviting people into their own close circle rather than have those same people barge in uninvited. The build-up of any relationship, in conversation or in one's social life, must always be a gradual process, more gradual with some people than with others.

Body language is as important as what you say: Never forget the importance of using body language to convey your own involvement with the speaker or listener. Body language in conversation is all-important since all conversation starts with a facial expression, usually a smile (sometimes even a scowl). It starts with an image which says clearly whether you are receptive to someone speaking to you and the response you get indicates the same. It is in the same mould as a firm handshake and without either, there is no prior indication whether there is any chemistry likely to flow at all. It is remarkable that many people still believe that an initially dour expression or a weak handshake has no effect at all on subsequent conversation. Conversely, either will direct the whole mood of what follows. Body language means eye contact, it means response, it means concentrating on the one person who is with you rather than showing (by your body language) that your mind is elsewhere. Certainly if someone is saying one thing and his body language is saying another, we will instinctively believe the body language first.

Your listener may be as insecure as you: Remember that in any social gathering, and even if you have no limitations yourself, there may well be others who feel insecure, who do not like to be among strangers, who have a fear that no-one will talk to them, and, if a conversation is opened, they will be nervous that they will have nothing to contribute. Some people *are* wary of talking to anyone new, and in such an environment they may well be looking for signs of confidence from you. It is an unreasonable reaction indeed if you think you are the only one in the room who feels unable to converse and communicate freely and easily. If you show enthusiasm when you meet someone, you will indicate your own interest in meeting them and show that you are prepared to be approachable – even if you are shy yourself.

Avoid the 'Have you heard the one about...': As a firm rule, unless you are a professional comedian, be wary of telling jokes. Almost regardless of their content, you will upset someone. It is, however, often the choice of those who find it difficult to find anything else to say.

First, a good stand-up comedy style is possessed by very few. If you are really that good, you will probably know it already (and can then get away with it), but if not, you are merely committing one of the first cardinal errors in conversation – promoting your own ego rather than working on the interests and expectations of your audience. If you are not sure which category you fall into, find a friend who is candid enough to tell you the truth and ask her opinion. Even then you might not get the right answer. The safest course is to avoid jokes altogether, since you will usually never find out the effect they are *really* having on your listeners. Remember, you will rarely be told if your jokes offend or are boring. Your listener will merely move on somewhere else.

Bad language is unacceptable: The other cardinal rule is to avoid the use of expletives. They are for those who have not learnt there are better and more descriptive words available. Similarly, avoid superlative expressions and over-expressive words. These are OK for Batman (or more correctly Robin), but do little for those who really wish to express themselves properly.

At this stage, it is worth reminding yourself that in any conversation it is easy to lose contact with your listener and this will usually be for one of four reasons.

1. You, as a speaker, may be boring, either in your tone of voice or in the lack of colour in your presentation. As discussed in the last chapter, these problems can be remedied by looking at the way the voice is used and the way enthusiasm and life can be brought into your own conversation.

2. The topic itself may be too complex or possibly even too basic or simple. Alternatively it may well have no general interest at all outside the world of the speaker. This comes back to using your empathy to discover what is the interest of your audience rather than what is the interest for you.

3. You may well be too forthright with your views so that your listener immediately dismisses you as someone with whom he can have a reasoned discussion. This comes back to the respect you must have for the values of others. The *real* conversationalist is the one who can anticipate such a problem and back away from it before it is recognised by others.

4. The listener may not be prepared, for one reason or another, to tune into your wavelength. He may already know the subject and realise that, for him, there is nothing new to be said. The other possibility is that he may have other matters on his mind and may not be prepared to concentrate on your own. Where this is a problem, your only option is to move on or switch to whatever subject *will* hold your listener. Your conversation will never succeed where you do not have a receptive ear.

Remember, when you react to the opinions of others, that you cannot expect everyone to agree with you, nor you always to be on *their* wavelength. It is often our reaction to opposing opinions, whether it be about the political situation, whether Chelsea have any chance of winning on Saturday, or whether God exists or he doesn't, that turns what should have been a normal discussion or conversation into an argument. It is this deliberate creation of barriers which often kills conversation rather than encourages it.

This does not mean that all our opinions need to be neutral just to avoid offending others since, in any conversation where you want to be persuasive, you *must* have the courage of your own convictions and be prepared to say things which on the face of it are not popular. However it is the *way* that such remarks are made that often labels a speaker arrogant or blind to other people's opinions.

For this reason also, anger has no part simply because it converts any conversation into an argument and determines from the outset that there will be no rapport between the speaker and the listener. That rapport is essential to nurture if you expect someone to listen to your views and possibly change her own as a result of what you have said. Anger not only has no part but also the type of remarks which create anger must also be eliminated. 'You must surely recognise that'; 'I find it hard to understand your view' and the classic 'with respect'; all serve to raise the hackles of your listener and ensure that he is less – not more – receptive to what you have to say. If necessary, pause and gather your thoughts before you continue so that you get back on an even keel. When you are emotionally disrupted you have little chance of talking in a controlled way.

You should also remember never to try to put down your listener, or indeed your customer, and regard his own views of no consequence. From your own experience you will probably not find it difficult to name certain political and union figures who have managed to alienate the listening public by their overbearing and arrogant disregard for any opinions which clashed with their own.

When looking at others and their skills in communicating, and indeed seeming at ease while doing so, it is interesting to see how people react with each other, and how they interact to ensure that what they say is as effectively received as possible. The really relaxed speakers will only talk when they have secured acceptance that someone is prepared to listen. In business, where you are in a relatively rigid hierarchy, this may even need to be a specific request such as 'May I say something?', but in social conversation it is true that permission is often sought in the same way, if only by an exchange of eye contact which asks and gets the same sort of answer. There are, of course, those who will speak regardless of whether that acknowledgment has been asked or given but a real acceptance of one sort or another is vital if you are to have a listener who is also a *willing* listener.

ESTABLISHING BOUNDARIES

We all have boundaries surrounding either our jobs or our personal lives and we may well, with different people, have different limits on how far we permit those speakers to overstep those boundaries. Some of us may not wish others to talk to us regarding our religious, political or even moral beliefs and it is as well to know what those limits are before we speak. Our views may be so strong (or egotistical) that we are not prepared to listen to others on that topic at all. For instance, on the subject of hunting, the pro-hunting lobby and the anti-hunting lobby have nothing even remotely in common to make discussion possible, and under such circumstances it would be sensible to avoid the topic altogether. In a business environment, we may have technical knowledge that we consider so unique that we are not prepared to accept advice from the less qualified, or indeed our listeners might have a similar knowledge so they are not prepared to accept advice from us. Those are both boundaries which are difficult to cross, and, once recognised, can be avoided since there is little point in trying to cross them. In business, the job description often defines those territories, but in social conversation, not only do we not have such a definition, but we are often dealing with people whom we do not know, and anyway, those boundaries can change daily.

We may well be living in personal situations where we are not prepared to let others intrude on our emotional territory. All these are circumstances where we can actually either refuse permission to discuss the topic or indicate less obviously that the topic is not welcome. Similarly, we might well indicate that an intrusion is acceptable with one person where we might not accept such an intrusion from another. It is essential as a speaker or conversationalist to recognise the signs and alter the subject to one that is acceptable. It is all very well to have a list of banned topics (or boundaries, if you like), for instance religion or politics, but there are many other areas where you can tread and cause offence simply because you are trespassing on ground where you should not be. Such trespass is regularly committed by those who are abrasive in their dealings with others, and few of us would need to look far to discover politicians who have caused their own downfall solely through their own failure to recognise the susceptibilities of others.

Equally in any conversation, once we have defined the limits which are acceptable, we need to have a set of rules which will help in ensuring that both listeners and speakers are satisfied that each has gained from what has been said, has enjoyed the environment in which it took place, and also accept that their own particular views have not been ignored or overriden.

■ No-one wants to be hectored and to feel that he is at the receiving end of a party political broadcast. If views are being submitted – and received – then that must be done in an atmosphere which represents cooperation rather than conflict.

■ Your comments must relate as far as possible to what the other party in any conversation has said and your views must not only reflect the replies that you get, but if necessary must be modified to adapt to them. If you merely regard an opposing view as a pause to get your breath to carry on further, then you will get as much acceptance from your listener as you gave to him.

■ If your conversation is to be *really* two-way, acknowledge constantly the other's point of view, disagreeing if you must. By acknowledgement you are at least making him aware that you have heard and absorbed his views.

■ If you wish to be really persuasive in your conversation, it is good advice to mix your opinions (which are essentially only subjective views) with specific facts which will be the same regardless of the speaker. 'The Second World War started in September 1939 [*fact*] but most people would agree [*opinion*] that it actually started over a year before.' Your listener will automatically agree with the fact element (he has no alternative), and will then more readily accept the opinion which follows. This type of reliance of opinion on fact is, for instance, a key element of all advertising and is just as useful in general conversation: 'Everyone is looking for an economical car' [*generally true*]; 'the **Wombat Trusty** will give that advantage to you' [*opinion*].

Because it forms such a regular part of our normal life, general conversation is rarely given the attention that it deserves and there is little doubt that many people search for artificial aids to assist them in 'finding things to talk about'. The advertising of items which are sold as 'conversation pieces' indicates how many people need a prop on which they can start and develop a conversation. Even the weather as a topic serves the same purpose.

Conversation should not, and certainly need not, be that difficult. The rules are not complicated but they certainly demand a degree of effort to ensure that they are recognised and your approach tailored to match up to them. Effective and persuasive talking is largely talking knowledgeably and confidently on topics in which others also have an interest. Get that right and you will already have established the essential of being a good conversationalist.

CHECKLIST

- Anticipate the problems and develop your self-confidence.

- Never talk on subjects on which your knowledge is limited.

- Avoid contentious subjects on which others have firm views.

- Always listen as much as you speak.

- Recognise the areas where you can lose listener contact.

6

The disciplines of business communication

It isn't that they cannot see the solution. It is that they cannot see the problem.

From *The Point of a Pin* by G K Chesterton.

In your business career, what you have to say and how you choose to say it, whether it be to customers or to colleagues, will be the controlling factors in whether you succeed or not. Even if you are highly skilled technically, but a poor communicator, I would venture to say that any success you have will be *in spite of* your lack of speaking skills, and that with proper communication at your command, you would achieve even greater success. One of your main objects in a business environment is to influence and control others and to persuade them that they need to follow your decisions. Often the achievement of that has little to do with the decisions themselves, but everything to do with the way that they are conveyed.

BUSINESS COMMUNICATION MAKES HIGHER DEMANDS

Remember that communicating in a business environment is very different from communicating socially, if only because in business you do not have the same ability to choose who you speak to, and you might well find yourself having to exchange conversation with others with whom you have little in common. Inevitably this makes the whole job of communicating a great deal harder.

In business, there is a range of areas where effective and persuasive conversation is vital:

- To get the job in the first place and to convince the prospective employer at the interview that it is in his best interests to employ *you* rather than someone else. In this your discipline must be rigid since the interviewer is assessing you not just on what you say, but also on whether you have the control and skill to give the exact information he is asking for and not expand into areas where he has no great concern.

- Once appointed, your job might well then be to employ staff and to convince the right person that he needs to bring his talents to you. In this role you need to develop a style which draws out from any candidate you are interviewing the real facts you are looking for. Since you are probably interviewing on your own territory, you hold most of the cards, and your job will be far more dedicated to prompting and listening than dominating the conversation yourself.

- In any position of responsibility you will have to communicate with your superiors who will need to know clearly and concisely what you are achieving for the salary you are being paid – possibly one of the most important skills of all since it is little use being effective at your job if you cannot communicate with others.

- Lastly, you need to be able to communicate with your subordinates so that they are either influenced to your way of thinking or informed effectively of new procedures. Here the enthusiasm with which you convey your message will be all important so that if you are successful, that same enthusiasm is generated down the line. The skill here needs to be developed so that you never appear to talk down to your subordinates but persuade them that your decisions are the right ones to follow.

Remember that most communication in business also has an element of selling, and needs the same care in its overall presentation. In some situations that element is stronger than in others, but there will always be some degree of persuasion even if that persuasion is merely to sell yourself to your listener as a person worth listening to.

Good English is rarely regarded as important

Unfortunately, for all the importance of getting our message across, the proper use of good English in business is probably one of the least regarded features in any business training programme. Virtually everyone receives some sort of training related to their specific job skills but the emphasis does not extend to ensuring a proficiency in communicating views and opinions to others. What the businessperson must spend time doing is analysing his or her own communication skills. How to issue instructions, how to convince others of the desirability of his plans, how to get a fair share of influence at meetings and to be able to run seminars and conferences that infuse others with his own enthusiasm. All this comes from an ability to speak with confidence and conviction, to express views with the expectation of having them accepted, and to make sure that as a salesman or manager, he is not only seen and heard, but also followed.

Effective communication is vital to the way that management translates its ideas into action down the line. It is vital to the way meetings become productive instead of time wasting. It is vital to ensure that participants secure from a conference or seminar a proper return for the cost of setting it up in the first place. It is also vital in any company's dealings with its customers and its final market.

So, for all the obvious importance, why is communication, both speaking and writing, not given the same emphasis as the other skills which are set for a company, and why is relatively little attention paid to communication skills when a prospective employee is being interviewed for a position with the company? Is it assumed that an acceptable level of skill will be there already; is it thought that if not there is nothing that can be done about it; or is it too indefinite a subject to insert into a company's training programme?

Good communication is rarely taught properly

The last assumption is probably the most likely one and it is certainly true that most companies back off from trying to teach others how to express themselves, working on the principle that, if possible, it is better to employ people with those talents in the first place. Sadly, many people are employed solely on their technical skills with no thought of whether they can convey or explain those skills to others. The reason is simply that while most employers will admit that the skills of making a speech or leading a business meeting are vitally important to any business professional, it is a fact that the average company employee probably spends 90 per cent of his time on his main responsibilities. Only 10 per cent of his time is spent trying to convince others, so that 10 per cent is given a low priority. However, if someone has technical knowledge and needs either to explain a decision or indeed transmit that knowledge to others, the quality of the actual communicating must be regarded as equally important as the content of what is being said. Whether that contact point is with subordinates or whether it is reporting up to a board meeting, there are cardinal rules you must follow if your words are to have any relevance to your audience.

So, what are you looking to change, and indeed, what are you looking to do that you do not do already?

■ *Can you disagree logically?*
Are you able to disagree with an opinion without appearing to attack the one who expresses that opposing opinion? Does what you say cause offence in others?

■ *Can you transmit unpopular views?*
Can you easily persuade others round to your way of thinking when maybe what you are expressing is initially a minority or unpopular view?

■ *Do you accept criticism evenly?*
Do you respond angrily if someone criticises your views and appears to be making a personal attack on you? Can you view that criticism objectively?

■ *Are you an active participant or merely an observer?*
Do you find that you contribute actively to company meetings or do you prefer to stand back and let others take the limelight and make the proposals?

■ *Can you command attention, and do you also give it?*
Do you find that people listen attentively to you and are you ready, whenever the occasion demands, to listen positively to them?

■ *Are you positive and confident in your own views?*
Do you have the skill to be positive in your presentation and put forward your ideas in a way that shows that *you* believe they are possible and viable? Or do you present ideas almost apologetically, and so transmit that negative approach to your audience?

MASTERING YOUR CONVERSATIONAL SKILLS

How can you achieve a mastery of conversation which will ensure that *you* are directing how a meeting is run, that *you* are deciding what course the conversation is taking, and that *you* are influencing the degree of authority that you can carry?

Present your views in a way acceptable to others: You must always speak with empathy, understanding the standpoint of the audience. As with selling, this empathy must still be the most important element – look at what he is saying to you so that you pick up the signals which tell you what *he* is looking for. This does not necessarily mean putting forward an opinion which secures immediate agreement but it certainly means expressing one that has a fair chance of being listened to.

Listening is as important as speaking: You will certainly need to improve your listening skills before you can even begin to speak with persuasion and conviction since, in order to speak convincingly, you must listen for the signals and then tailor your way of talking to suit the listener. This adjustment is obviously more important in a selling career than in general conversation since you will often be placed in front of someone you have not had the chance to evaluate before. In the words of Norman R Augustine, 'Often one hears the remark, "He talks too much", but when did anyone last hear the criticism, "He listens too much"?'.

The pace at which you transmit is vital: All discussions, meetings and even general conversation tend to lose their value when opinions are expressed too fast for the participants to absorb. That value declines simply because the speakers are determined to establish their right to speak and are not prepared to give equal importance to listening to others. The moment this happens, the effectiveness of your own conversation, and the willingness of others to listen to it, declines to a level where it hardly matters what you *do* say since a gap has been created between yourself and your listeners. For this reason, it is essential that you control the speed of the conversation. This can be achieved in a number of ways:

1. You can review your own thoughts and go back on what you have said previously.

2.   You can summarise someone else's opinions to ensure that you have understood and also to slow down the flow of new opinions being expressed.

3.   You can remove any anger or irritation which generated the increase in pace of the conversation in the first place. This can very often be achieved by offering a compromise in your own standpoint.

4.   You can discover the elements which are taking a listener ahead of the others and try to eliminate factors which may well be more important for one listener than for another. We all look at topics in different ways and sometimes the excessive ardour, or intractability, of one person can destroy the chances of a sensible discussion on that topic.

5.   If you are in a formal meeting and you are in the chair, you are probably in a position to control the speed yourself. If you are merely part of a group, whether formal or informal, that control will demand more effort since others will regard their opinions as being as important as your own. However, if you are to become persuasive yourself, that control is just what you need to achieve. Act as a chairman, even in your social conversation, and you will be recognised as someone who contributes to the easy running of any discussion. Any good discussion demands such a control and that is why at dinner parties a good host or hostess will try to include someone who is able to stimulate and guide the content of what is being said.

Two-way conversation is a two-way responsibility!: Beware of any conversation or discussion that becomes one-sided, whichever way the emphasis is leaning. All communication must be two-way to be effective and without adequate and effective response, conversation cannot be properly effective.

Match your content to the capabilities of your audience: Your presentation must match the level of all your audience. This means analysing the competence of your listeners in a field where you may be an expert and talking to them in a language they can relate to. In simple terms this obviously means avoiding the use of jargon but it also means not talking over their heads so that they are unable to make a sensible appraisal of your opinions. If this means leaving out some of the more technical arguments, then so be it.

Never speak without having an object in view: You must know before you start what you are seeking to achieve. While few would deny this, it is a fact that many meetings and conferences are held with only a hazy idea of what the final objective is and consequently the agenda, or the programme, tends to drift without real purpose. For example, in a meeting, good persuasive speaking means understanding, in your own mind, what are the main points that you are trying to express, and outlining them clearly to the audience so that they understand why you are talking. Listeners who get bored with a speaker talking round the subject are the same listeners who will swiftly recognise someone who is keen to get to the purpose of the discussion, and who tells them ahead what that purpose is.

You are looking for acceptance: In any presentation, whether it be a committee meeting or a conference, you should still aim to secure the 'yes' response the whole time. It may well only be the nodding of heads (hopefully not asleep) which tells you that the listener is on your side, but questions should be sent out, usually to the chairman in a formal meeting, which will encourage a response. The more of those responses that you have coming back, the more you will have the audience swinging to your side or at the very least understanding the message that you are putting across. It is only by handling your argument in this way that you will discover whether you need to work harder on your persuasive powers.

Be prepared for objections: If you are planning to control any meeting to your advantage, you must become more skilful in dealing with opponents who try to knock you off balance. Know your subject and deal with opposition in a firm but non-abrasive way. People *can* be persuaded, but rarely can they be brow-beaten. If they eventually agree, it might well be under duress and not with the cooperation that you would have preferred. Speaking with conviction is *convincing* the listener to make his own decision, not compelling him to accept your own.

Look for the signals of agreement: Try to pick up clues along the way which might show that your listener is either swinging to your side or away from you. These clues may be verbal or take the form of body language. Annoyance in a listener is usually obvious yet many speakers will continue regardless. It is essential, if need be, to change your approach once those signals have been read so that once more the recipient can be brought back on to your wavelength. Work out for yourself how *you* respond to someone who is alienating you by his approach and you will soon be able to recognise the same reaction in others.

Be willing to change direction: It is also essential to be prepared to change your own view or concept if someone else's views are more persuasive than your own. The assumption that you are always right and it is merely a matter of talking long enough to persuade everyone else is not only arrogant but is also unproductive in a situation where compromise is often the result everyone is looking for. You must be prepared to acknowledge that another's view might have more credibility than your own, or even that he has prepared his arguments more effectively than you have. The whole object of a conversation or a discussion is to submit suggestions, proposals or opinions, and, unless you intend to be dictatorial, you must then be prepared to alter your own view if the response you get warrants it.

Use humour sparingly: Finally, as I have mentioned previously, beware of becoming the company joke teller. There are those who cannot resist the opportunity of displaying their talents whenever the occasion arises and so destroy their chances of being taken seriously when a different situation presents itself. Unfortunately you cannot choose when you are to be taken seriously and when you are to be the comic.

GIVE AND TAKE

All communication, in business or elsewhere, comes back to presenting your views, and accepting the views of others, in a way that leaves both sides happy that they have secured at least a part of what they want, whether that part is agreement, understanding, or merely the fact that someone else has listened and absorbed their views. Most factors which are barriers to that understanding are created by those who are not prepared to listen to others and who believe that communication need not necessarily be two-way. There is all the difference in the world between conversation (and communication) which is assertive and conversation which is arrogant. The former gets what you want and leaves the recipient reasonably pleased with what has been achieved. The latter sometimes gets what you want also, but does so in a way that leaves the other person resentful.

The whole object in communication in business is to get your message across clearly, and, where the message may be an unpopular one, to get it across with as little resentment as possible. This may often mean the use of skilful explanation and persuasion. Rarely, if you are in a position of authority, will you be told why you fail to communicate effectively and it will often be left to you alone to analyse your own performance and to decide whether being persuasive might have more effect than being dogmatic. The rules for being persuasive are the same as those you use when you are away from the office. The difference is that in your business environment, the consequences of not getting it right are far greater.

CHECKLIST

- Business communication makes higher demands.

- Ideas are only as good as the way they are transmitted.

- Command authority when you speak.

- Create a bridge between you and your listener.

- Remember the dangers of one-way conversation.

- Always be prepared to compromise or change your opinions.

7

Negotiate with skill

Persuasive negotiation is the art of winning and at the same time leaving the buyer convinced that he also has won

Sian Bronham, 1930

While the previous chapter has concentrated on the general business aspect of ensuring your conversation is effective and persuasive, most of us would agree that in a business environment the most important persuasive powers must lie with the sales force who talk with the customers. In this chapter we will analyse the specific problems that face the salesman and how the rules outlined in this book must be used to make his everyday job more effective. This chapter is not a complete bible on selling – other books cover the subject far more comprehensively than that – but it is a guide on how conversation can be made easier, can be made to sound more convincing and can be made more persuasive.

THE PRINCIPLES OF PERSUASIVE NEGOTIATION

Persuasive selling comes back to the art of making it seem so effortless that the buyer is not aware of it. It is the art of negotiating in such a way that both sides feel that they have each, as far as possible, won as many of the points as they thought possible. It is the art of tuning people in to us, and we to them, so that they want to deal with us and they do not feel dominated or threatened. This is what the Americans call the 'win-win' situation and it is always the basis of successful negotiating. It must be achieved in a disciplined way and is based on the following principles:

- *What is the other person looking for?*
  Initially you must establish a range of criteria, the most important being what the other side actually wants. This is the same whether you are dealing with a complaint, a sale, or whatever. It is a sad fact that often the question is never asked. Proper negotiation is analysing what the other side is expecting, since two different customers may not both be looking for the same thing – the best price, the most efficient machine or whatever other element is important. You cannot negotiate until you know what those factors are.

- *Know your own requirements*
  You need to set out your own demands and ensure that you lodge those demands in the mind of the other person so that everyone is aware what gap there may be between the two points of view. Until you know what this gap actually is, there is little point in negotiating at all.

- *Collect information*
  With the gap in mind, you have to secure information. The more you probe and the more facts you discover, the more you will reveal details which will affect the criteria you have already established in the first stage. Your aim will be to be one step ahead of the other party so that you can anticipate problems, questions and answers before they actually arrive. Information is not difficult to get but you *do* need to ask.

- *Look for compromise*
  You then need to analyse where there is a compromise so that you know what you can give away, what you *need* to give away, and what the other party can give away. All negotiation eventually ends in compromise, and the one who has that compromise clearly outlined has all the advantages in knowing where he wants to be. You can then work on the skills which will get you there.

Negotiators are restricted by conditions

A good negotiator should accept that the following concepts will control all his actions:

- He must accept that all negotiation is a two-way business and that both sides need to feel that they are equally involved. This means that both must feel they are benefiting from the negotiation that has taken place. Each must care, or at least appear to care, about the standards and needs of the other, so that both consider, at the end, that they have secured as fair a deal as they could have got.

■ A good negotiator must be prepared to leave the negotiations whenever he believes he should. One of the cardinal errors is to feel a necessity to talk through to a definitive conclusion, regardless of concessions given, even when that conclusion may well not be what you want. If the buyer has such a deadline and is under pressure to make a swift decision, then so much the better since he is then at his weakest, but as a seller you should not feel compelled to make an unfavourable compromise simply because there is a limit on your own time.

■ Good negotiation demands the recognition that everyone is different and therefore demands a different approach. This should force us to be sympathetic to many varying points of view and adapt our own approach to match those differences. A head-on argument rarely results in a mutually satisfactory solution.

■ Remember that empathy in conversation is saying what you believe your listener wants you to say. Most of the time we say what *we* want with little regard or anticipation of how it will be received. Persuasive conversation means removing as many risks as possible of being abrasive. Being in tune with your listener and getting on his wavelength will help in making you both an acceptable speaker and a convincing one.

RULES FOR SUCCESSFUL NEGOTIATION

The above concepts form the basis of any good negotiator and with that framework in mind, it will be useful to draw up a list of rules which will help you conform to that basis in your own environment.

Your first job is to maintain the interest

Retaining the interest of a listener is the platform of *all* successful negotiation. Fail to recognise that, or fail to notice that you have lost that interest means that the remainder of your communication, and the nature of the benefits you are offering, will fall on deaf ears. It is vital that you train yourself to recognise negative body language and realise when other factors may be distracting your prospect so that you are not wasting your time.

Presenting benefits is still the golden rule

When speaking to persuade, it is well to remember to present the benefits of what you are saying rather than the features. This means outlining the advantages you are offering by suggesting those features in the first place. If you are promoting the advantages of a redesigned production line, you may believe this will achieve a better turnaround of product. To an accountant the benefit will be a higher profit. To a personnel manager, the benefit might be a happier and less stressed workforce. To the works manager, a faster production line and to the union representative, a better paid workforce. The sales director will obviously see the same machine improvement as a chance to come out with a more competitively priced product. To every one of these people you must state your arguments in a different way so that each is convinced of the benefit for him- or herself. That is using your empathy to analyse your listeners so each hears you in the way he wants to. Speak with conviction so that people hear you with conviction.

Know the names of those you are talking to

Always address people by their names and use them regularly. This means, particularly if you are talking with a number of people at one time, ensuring that you collect (and remember) names when you first meet people so that you can deal with them on a more personal basis later. The really persuasive business person uses names constantly to reinforce and direct what is being said. People like to think you have taken the trouble to remember who they are. If you don't believe me, think how you react when an unknown cashier at a strange bank actually reads your name off a cheque and then uses that same name to thank you for your service. It is easy and is also good selling. Remember that a failure to remember a name is usually little to do with a poor memory. It is usually related to the fact that you did not really listen to it in the first place.

Project your enthusiasm!

You need to be constantly aware of the effect you have on others. Do you project sincerity or are you possibly so bored with your product that you fail to generate enthusiasm in others? Speaking persuasively demands that you maintain the level of enthusiasm in your own presentation, whether you feel that enthusiasm or not.

Suit your approach to your natural personality

Whatever you do in your conversation, aim for it to be natural to your own personality, and not an approach which you find difficult to make. An initial neutral approach will enable you to take more time in assessing your customer to discover what his own demands are likely to be. You can then adjust to them if the situation demands it.

Thrive on objections

Welcome objections and use them as your launch platform for any negotiation. Without objections you have little idea of what reaction you are getting and have consequently little idea of where your negotiation should be leading. A good objection always makes negotiating easier; indifference always makes it more difficult. The principle of agreeing with objections still stands – always follow agreement with your qualification. For example, 'I agree that delivery is later than you would like, but in the long term you will be getting machines to the right specification and not accepting a compromise.' Without the objection in the form it was presented, you would not have had the opportunity to refute it by reasserting the benefits.

You should, of course, always check the validity of any objection, a price range or any other negative reaction and find out whether it is a valid objection or not. It is simply a matter of saying, for example, 'If I were to find you exactly what you are looking for at well above the price you have indicated as your maximum, would you still be interested in looking at it?' If the answer is 'Yes', then you know that in this instance the price restriction is not as rigid as was previously indicated.

Sometimes you may even be presented with an objection which is not really a problem at all but one which you can happily concede on, so long as you get, say, the 5 per cent discount you were requesting previously. You finish up securing a real advantage and losing a concession which was of no great consequence.

Look for body language

The good negotiator will back good conversation with a body language which conveys warmth. Eye contact is essential if you are to gain credibility. Later we will discuss the problems this presents when we have no eye contact, as in telephone selling.

Good listening is as important as good speaking

Remember that persuasive talking is impossible if good listening does not precede it. Time and time again communication breaks down because people have not taken the trouble to listen to each other. You cannot be persuasive if you do not know where persuasion is likely to succeed.

Compromise is the basis of good negotiation

Remember that compromise is the strongest form of negotiation since both sides then believe that they have achieved what they were looking for. If, for example, you are selling a second-hand television, your conversation will take the form of suggesting a price which the purchaser may then question, so prompting a counter offer from yourself, and so on. Eventually an agreement is reached, neither side having achieved the original standpoint. Satisfactory negotiation itself must always be a compromise of views, again with both sides possibly altering their original views.

Price negotiation should be the most controlled of all

Always be careful when making the first offer to negotiate on the price. The first indication that price is, or should be, negotiable must come from the buyer, since you are then conceding to his demands rather than varying your initial set of criteria. Again, proposals to lower the price, or 'split the difference' if that is the situation, should always come from the buyer rather than the seller, since the advantage is then left with the seller to negotiate further to secure what he wants. Do it the other way round and you have shown your willingness to climb down from your standpoint before you have agreed a deal.

Keep your options open

Never nail down all the other issues in a deal and then leave one particular point on which to agree. This ensures there must be a winner and a loser since neither of you have anything left to negotiate with. The principle of always trading one concession for a second one to balance it is both effective in getting to your final close but also guarantees the aim of leaving both sides happy with what they have achieved. Remember that by exchanging points, you will have upgraded the value of what you are giving away by making it seem more difficult to agree to it.

Use silence as a negotiating tool

Always remember that one of your most powerful techniques must be the use of silence to persuade your listener to make a decision. This means making a proposition, or a trial close, and then leaving the buyer to make the next move without further prompting from yourself. The longer that pause takes before he reacts, the more likely he will respond in your favour. If, having made your proposition, you then continue with further reasons why a decision should be made, you will fail in getting the definitive answer you are looking for. In the words of Elizabeth Bowen, 'Silences have a climax when someone has to speak'. Make sure that person is not you.

Maintain your own authority

Be wary of using the stratagem of telephoning someone else to give you the necessary authority to extend the offer you have made. While it is recommended in many sales manuals as a way out when the negotiation appears to have got bogged down, you immediately put yourself in a position where you throw away your own authority and convince the buyer that whatever you offer, there is a better deal lurking somewhere round the corner. A good sales manager will give that extended authority, whether related to price, delivery or discounts, direct to his salesmen, encouraging them by commission or whatever to use the authority with skill. The buyer is then aware that there are no alternative options available to him elsewhere within your company and that any negotiation must be conducted with the salesman in front of him.

Be wary of being over-aggressive

We all know that a buyer should be reluctant and not over-enthusiastic about the deal. A seller should do the same and never appear to be over-enthusiastic to sell, regardless of how attractive the proposal put to him may be. It is essential that this reluctance to sell is apparent since a buyer will soon realise if his first offer was accepted more quickly than it should have been. Both sides should always start with asking more, and offering less, than they really expect to get. You may well think this to be a time-wasting game, but if you fail to do it and have no movement on your price, your buyer will have no satisfaction if he has not been able to do anything to secure a better deal for himself, even though he may have secured the best deal which was available.

Negotiate face to face

Finally, *never* negotiate by telephone. You lose all the advantages of body language since a high proportion of communication is non-verbal and you immediately lose all the visual signs as to whether the negotiation is acceptable or not.

INFLUENCE AND AWARENESS

Power negotiating is a gradual process of getting stage-by-stage agreement to whatever proposal you are submitting and is the principle of getting commitments down the line to positive decisions as they arise. This not only resolves the smaller issues which move the matter to a conclusion, but also gets the 'Yes' answers which help towards the big decision at the end. Anything other than a gradual process will seem to dominate the buyer and make him feel that he is not part of the deal which is being constructed.

Persuasive selling and persuasive speaking involves total understanding of the customer, a choice of words and language that a buyer or a listener can relate to, and it means making a presentation which maintains a constant interest throughout. It means eliminating abrasion, either in vocabulary or manner, and it is the ability to convey sincerity and enthusiasm. It means creating the situation where both sides believe they have secured for themselves the best deal which was available. You can even, if you wish, praise the other person for his negotiating skills since most people welcome the indication that they are hard negotiators and then become further convinced that they have secured the best deal they could.

But, most of all, powerful negotiation means controlling the scene and knowing that you have the ability to influence others in the way they react to you. A development of that power means a constant awareness that there are improvements to be made and to develop skills whenever the opportunity arises. There must be a conscious effort in the mind of the speaker to avoid the mistakes which he knows to be wrong but which, in spite of that, he still commits every day. There is only one way to negotiate and that is in the style that the customer expects. Persuasive selling and persuasive speaking matches that demand.

CHECKLIST

■ Persuasive selling leaves both sides pleased with the outcome.

■ Know the options and alternatives open to any negotiator.

■ Understand the discipline needed to improve your negotiating skills.

■ Real power negotiation must be a gradual process.

■ Powerful negotiating means that *you* control the situation.

8

Talking to a wider audience

Make sure that you have finished speaking before your audience have finished listening.

Dorothy Sarnoff

Being at ease and talking to one person, to your friends, or indeed to your customers, is one thing. Talking to a larger audience presents more difficulties since you immediately lose the ability to 'home in' accurately on the empathy of your listeners and you are compelled to talk in a far more general way. You cannot, in these circumstances, easily alter your presentation to suit every listener and merely have to aim at pleasing as many as possible.

In speaking to a wider audience many other factors enter into the fray and the importance of stance and conveying your own self-confidence comes high on the list of attributes you must encourage. You are interpreted as much by your words as how you say them and unless you are careful, your body language may be saying one thing while your words are saying another. You will be watched as much as heard and it is certainly not difficult to destroy the conviction of your speech by an unconscious gesture. Developing characteristics which convey your own feelings are almost as important as working on the words that you use and there are few who would not admit that apprehension in addressing a large gathering encourages actions which indicate our nervousness.

SELF-ASSURANCE IS THE KEY

Many people who quite happily talk on a one-to-one basis become tongue-tied when it comes to addressing a wider audience, even to the point where they are physically unable to address a meeting, regardless of whether they are talking to strangers or their own colleagues. In addition they find it a problem to analyse the reason for their difficulties since they will argue that they have adequate vocabulary, and indeed use it in other more private applications, and also have adequate self-confidence in everything else they do.

The reason is really quite simple. Public speaking demands a series of techniques which is not demanded in everyday conversation. Without confidence that you have acquired those techniques, you have a high chance of failing. Learn those techniques and satisfy yourself that you can use them effectively and you will be able to use your conversational skills as easily in public as your probably already do in a normal face-to-face discussion.

Common fears

In public speaking, the most important characteristic to develop is your mental attitude. Few would deny that fear of failure is the main reason why people prefer not to speak in public at all, and is the reason why many amateur speakers feel the need to apologise even before they start: 'You know, I'm not really used to this sort of thing,' or the disastrous 'Unaccustomed as I am to public speaking'. That fear is generated by the thought of running out of words, and while it is always a risk that you can dry up in your speech if you are continually looking for the appropriate word, it is nevertheless easier if you approach the sense of what you are saying from a different way so that you are not tying yourself to a set series of words which you have learnt by heart. Sometimes, when you are stuck for words, your listener may even provide the right ones (although it might be too optimistic to rely on that as a matter of course).

The other main fear is that you will run out of ideas before you run out of time to present them. You will *always* be nervous and lack confidence if you have nothing to say. You will always be full of confidence if you have prepared well and have no worries that you cannot adequately fill the time that you have been allocated. It is not fear of speaking that concerns you but it *is* fear of your own lack of preparation and possible inadequacy when you actually stand up. Prepare well and there will be little need for you to lack confidence at all. Certainly you will feel apprehension – even in the theatrical profession most actors or actresses are nervous prior to a performance. Although still confident of their own ability, their adrenalin (and nervousness, if you like) is stimulated as a result of the excitement of what they are doing, and they would probably agree that without it they would achieve only a mediocre result. In conditions where you are expected to speak in a genuinely impromptu way, virtually anyone will be disinclined to get up on his feet to speak and of all factors which contribute to the right attitude, the knowledge that you have adequate material to hand is probably the most important of all. Once you have that at your fingertips, you can begin to cultivate the characteristics which make a good speaker into a *really* good speaker.

The audience is probably on your side

Probably one of the best confidence boosters is that, in principle, the audience to whom you are speaking want you to succeed. The subject interests them, otherwise they would not be there, and generally speaking they will be prepared to reach out to meet you so that you will all gain from the occasion. Your listeners are *not* waiting for you to collapse or to make a mistake. Remember that the audience is probably made up of like people to yourself who will be sympathetic to what you are aiming to do, and are possibly even glad that they are not up there speaking themselves. You will, of course, need to present your material in a format which they will enjoy and this reaffirms my second point, that you must use empathy in understanding how the audience wants to receive you. It is also worthwhile remembering that most listeners have, through bitter experience, become used to bad speakers and unimaginative, ill-prepared presentations. If you, through your own expertise, offer them something even marginally better than that, they will be prepared to listen.

Know the geography of where you are going to speak

In talking to a wider audience, one of the best ways of raising your own level of self-confidence, and indeed one of the best ways of ensuring that it all goes well in the performance, is to check out as early as you can the physical attributes of the place where you are going to speak, and so destroy the apprehension that there might be unexpected problems later in the day. Often it will be only a few hours prior to the meeting that you will get the chance to check it out at all (and sometimes not even then), but the knowledge that everything matches up to what you want is invaluable. It goes without saying that you should arrive well before the time you actually need to be there so that you have time to relax and gather your thoughts before you are called upon to speak. Here are a few checkpoints:

■ Can you see everybody, and can they see you?

■ If you are using a microphone, does it work and is the lead long enough if you need to move over to a flipboard or a screen?

■ Can the room be darkened, should it be necessary?

■ Are the acoustics right or does the electronic equipment squeal whenever the volume is turned up to the desired level? Make sure at the same time that any audio and visual equipment, your own or theirs, is working properly and can be loaded with *your* visuals.

■ If the bulb on the projector blows, is there another one to hand, or would the whole speech be a disaster if it was not backed by the slides you have brought? Better to have a second projector to hand if that is the case.

All these physical accessories to your speech are pitfalls which can go wrong and if you ensure, as far as possible, that they will not go wrong, then you can concentrate on your prime job which is the speech itself.

Aides-mémoires

During your actual speech (depending of course on the type of pre-sentation it is) you will need notes. Of course it is important that you do not plan to read your speech notes rather than use them as a reminder. Read your speech word for word and your audience will soon realise that they are not being spoken to at all but are simply being read to and will react to the reading in the same way as if they were listening to the radio. Few people are either accustomed to reading in public, or indeed are good at it, and by reading your speech you will be tearing down the bridge between you and your audience, a bridge that as a speaker you should be trying to create. If you have to read and so concentrate more on a correct following of the text rather than on the importance of the topic, you will, at an early stage, lose contact with your audience.

However, on occasion you might well have to read verbatim, possibly if you are presenting someone else's work. If you are forced into this you should bear in mind the following rules.

■ Check the script well beforehand and make sure that a paragraph does not continue from one page to another. Turning a page mid-sentence while the audience waits in anticipation of what you have to say ensures that you direct their attention from what you are saying to the paper you are reading from.

■ Always insist that the writing or typing is double spaced. If you *do* lose your way it is easier to find it again if there is not a mass of type to search through.

■ Mark pauses wherever your rehearsal decides pauses should be. Marking will remind you that the pauses you plan are as important as the words you plan. In any script designed for reading, dashes should be as plentiful as full stops, and will help you control the all-important speed of delivery.

■ *Never* pass out copies of your speech to the audience beforehand. To do it afterwards is no problem, but passing out copies before-hand merely ensures that your audience, who can read faster than you can talk, will be reading it well ahead of you.

■ Always ensure that new ideas are on new pages. That will tend to match up with your own change of gear when you introduce a new heading and aspect of your talk.

■ Commit to memory as much as possible and actually read as little as possible. Remember that whenever you are looking at your script, you are not looking at your audience. Loss of eye contact must take away from your ability to be persuasive.

READING SPEECHES – THE PITFALLS

There are, of course, reasons why people insist on reading their speeches rather than using notes to keep them on track but generally these reasons come from a lack of proper preparation. This in turn leads the speaker to believe that a speech presented without word-for-word notes is certain to dry-up or to be disorganised. There is only one way to avoid that problem and that is to be organised in the first place so that you know what you are going to say, and then have a prompt system, on cards or whatever, to bring you back on course if you should go astray. *Never read*, unless you are presenting a paper prepared by someone else.

Reading your own speech when it is not necessary is undesirable for a good many reasons:

■ You cannot sound sincere when your main concern is to read ahead of what you are actually saying.

■ You will not develop your own self-confidence if you are totally reliant on a sheet of paper, written by you or someone else, which provides the ammunition for you.

■ You cannot use physical expressions or movements if you are tied (metaphorically speaking) to a lectern.

■ You cannot maintain any real eye-to-eye contact with your audience if you are working continuously from a script.

In the House of Commons and the House of Lords, speeches, by tradition, cannot be read, with the exception of reports submitted by others. These are presented at the Despatch Box by the Minister concerned. Notes are permitted, reading is not, and it is as well to use the same rule in your own speaking. Read a quotation by all means, this merely assumes that you are giving an *accurate* quotation rather than a general summary of someone else's views. On these occasions you should even make your reading obvious since the audience will appreciate the research you have done to unearth the quotation for their benefit.

MAKING YOUR SPEECH NOTES

Cards are the only practical answer for making notes. The reason is simple enough: paper is larger and has a tendency to rustle, so creating a diversion which you can well do without. With cards, even if you drop them they are easily reassembled and they do not distract the audience so much as reams of paper which always indicate a lengthy presentation ahead. To avoid cards falling out of order, use a tail tag – the sort with a plastic or metal 'T' at each end – to hold them together. Even if cards are numbered they would need to be re-sorted unless tags are used. In addition, by using a tag, secondary points can easily be added at the last minute. Remember that anything which avoids things going wrong – so giving you greater confidence – is worth doing. Another valuable piece of advice is that whatever the size or type of cards that you use, prepare a duplicate set and keep them separate from the others. In the event of the worst happening and your main notes go adrift, you at least have a replacement set to fall back on. You would probably not be the first person to arrive at Kennedy Airport in New York while your baggage and notes are being processed at Reykjavik in Iceland!

The cards should be small, about 6 × 4 inches at most, and should be clearly visible 30 inches away. With a good lectern, that is where they should probably be anyway. As prompt cards, they should contain only single *key* words which will jog your mind into remembering paragraphs and sentences. Don't write those sentences in full as that will automatically encourage you to read the cards rather than glance at them.

Many books tell you that you should always speak without notes since the use of them forces you to look away from your audience. I would certainly accept the truth of the second part of that statement, but I believe that notes are a small price to pay for having available, in some written form, what you intend to say. By all means raise your eyes from those notes as often as you can and for as long periods as you can, but keep track of your speech the whole time by using your notes as your reminder. As you get more proficient, your notes will certainly become more abbreviated and summarised, but believe me, your confidence can be easily shattered if you have no way of falling back on an *aide-mémoire* when your own memory deserts you. Speakers who use no notes at all are marvellous to hear, but they are rarities and you will probably fail if you try to emulate them.

Even if you write out your entire script and rehearse it that way (and you will probably find that initially you need to) *always* practise without your script before you actually go in to speak. Many people practise with their scripts up to the last minute simply because the script is there, and they are then surprised that they lack confidence when they make the speech without it. It is also advisable to limit the way you write out any speech in full beforehand since that method presents you with a number of disadvantages:

1. You are automatically trying to remember each phrase and sentence and this demands a level of concentration which is likely to increase any nervousness you may already have.

2. If you are trying to remember a written script rather than working more freely from a set of notes which are acting as a framework, your speech will always tend to sound more stilted than it should. A

spoken presentation (and indeed an impromptu one, if that is what you are presented with) will always be more informal and acceptable to an audience than one which has obviously been pre-written.

3.   If, when using a full script as your basis, your memory *should* fail you, you have little else to fall back on. The impromptu alternative you then have available is bound to be both unrehearsed and unprofessional.

PRESENTATION IS ALL-IMPORTANT

Remember that when you are speaking in public there are a number of characteristics you must encourage and which should command equal importance with the words themselves.

Speak at a pace that others can absorb

First, the speed of your delivery is all-important since you must adapt to your whole audience, and that means matching up to the most disadvantaged of your audience – an elderly, slower person, or one who is hard of hearing. Almost without exception, your speed of delivery should be considerably slower than you really believe to be necessary. And *never* ask 'Can you hear me at the back?' You will only get a shouted 'No' from the humorists in your audience and you should already have decided for yourself whether they can hear or not and have adjusted your presentation accordingly.

Address the back of the room

In a large room, speak to the back of it and then assume that the person standing there is almost deaf (he might well be). Rarely will anyone complain that he cannot hear, but if you make the error of speaking too softly, you can be sure that the resultant buzz of conversation from those out of earshot will disrupt the concentration of those closer to you.

Use pauses skilfully to create impact

You must regard as vital the way you use pauses for effect so that your audience has time to react to what you have said. This means using pauses and silence in as disciplined a way as you use your words, bearing in mind that a well-placed pause increases the impact of when you next begin to speak.

You are talking personally to each person in the room

Remember that you are never speaking to a hall full of people. You are speaking to a large number of separate individuals who each demand the same kind of attention you would give to an individual on his own. A difficult task indeed but a skill which separates the true professional from the one who puts in little effort to get his message across. In the words of Charles Reade, 'Always speak as though there were only one person in the hall whom you had to convince.'

Total preparation is an essential rule

Make sure that you have prepared all the details you need. It must be assumed that you know your subject, otherwise you would not have been asked to speak. If you have been asked to research and report, then it is assumed that by the time you begin speaking you *will* be knowledgeable. Either way, the knowledge should be there and pre-planned in your head. There are many people who consider themselves so well briefed on a topic they do not consider it necessary to do anything but play it by ear as they go along. If that is to be your option, you had better be a naturally born professional speaker. But be warned: there are not many of them about.

Know your listeners and their demands

Do not even agree to speak unless you are informed about the audience you will have on front of you. Imagine a musician who is asked to play 'music' to a group of people. His first job must be to find out their taste so that, however well he plays, he can provide music that they like. The same must apply to any speech although a rigid subject matter may only leave you with a choice of how it is presented. With any audience you must talk at their level of knowledge, not above it so that they do not understand, nor below it so that they feel they know the subject better than you. Difficult with a large audience, but that should certainly be your aim, and sometimes that will mean altering your own presentation as you go along so that you adapt to the conditions which you are presented with. Just because you are an expert on a subject yourself does not mean that the audience are as well informed, and yet many presentations are put together on the skills of the speaker and not the abilities of the audience. Never expect people to adapt to you since they will refuse to do so and you will surely lose their concentration and interest.

Have an objective and be constantly aware of it

Know your objective in talking. Decide beforehand what attitude of mind you want your listeners to leave with and work backwards from that. If your objective is for them to leave enthusiastically prepared to enter a new sales campaign, decide what convincing factors they need to achieve that and then ensure that your talk provides them. Determine whether the aim is to instruct, entertain or persuade. Decide what the audience actually wants. Are you trying to educate them when all they want is entertainment? There *is* often a difference between the speaker's view of the objective and the objective seen from the angle of the listener. They should certainly match up as closely as possible but it is making hard work to try to bend the audience to your own interpretation of what is needed.

Work to a clear framework

Bear in mind that a good structure is important, not only for yourself so that you can follow it easily, but also for the audience so that they can swiftly attune to it. Once 'in' they can be more easily encouraged to follow it so that the whole talk appears to have an overall structure that they can recognise. They will, of course, occasionally lose contact but it is far easier for them to rejoin you if you are following the pattern which is in their minds.

Retain control of your audience

Do not allow questions during your presentation, unless it has been designed on a question and answer basis. Obviously you can have queries at the end, but it is unfair to you and your audience to disrupt your own presentation by answering a question which might well be answered automatically later in the talk. If a question should arise unexpectedly, make a note of it and say you will deal with it at the end. The only other alternative is to let the audience control your own programme – a certain recipe for disaster. It is a simple enough arrangement to ensure that the audience know when questions are to be put by you or the chairperson making it clear beforehand. For total peace of mind, it is well to avoid the phrase 'Are there any questions?' altogether since by doing so you may well project yourself into an area which you have not planned or, even worse, you may get no response at all. By eliminating question time and ensuring that the chair of a meeting does not upstage you by making the offer on your behalf, you retain control of the way your speech is handled and received. Aim to keep that control for yourself.

Body language is important but keep it neutral

Remember that your posture is important but that a negative stance will be noticed far less than an exaggerated one. It is not necessary to wave your arms to express a point, and indeed that will affect the audience's concentration. Keep your hands empty, except perhaps for your card notes, but otherwise don't use your arms at all. If you don't believe how excessive movements can distract, think how we laugh and even caricature our European friends who continually wave their arms to emphasise their point of view. It is a way of showing expression on the continent but has the opposite effect over here. There should certainly be some body movement but all expressions and gestures should be as moderate as when we are talking face-to-face with one other person. Similarly, do not constantly move your weight from one foot to the other. By all means move, but make those moves rare so that they are used to full effect. A further rule concerns your hands. One hand in your pocket is acceptable. Two hands are not.

The second piece of advice regarding your posture is *never* sit, whatever the invitation to do so. Standing gives you authority; it enables you to control your audience and enables the audience to see you. Always speak from a standing position and if possible from a position which is as centrally placed for as many of the audience as possible.

Alcohol is for the audience

If you plan to be the speaker that others will listen to, leave the alcohol until you have finished. It will do nothing for your skills, or indeed your nervousness, although you might think so at the time, and will diminish your ability to monitor the audience to decide whether they are with you or not. Be aware also that while you, hopefully, have kept off the alcohol your audience may well not have done the same, and their concentration might be that more difficult to hold.

Joke-telling is not for the amateur

Use humour skilfully and *never* tell a joke which is not relevant. Remember that humour and jokes are not the same. You may get a good response from the audience but when the laughter has stopped, if the topic was not relevant to the general speech, you will need to spend time getting back to your original theme before you can get started again. If you do tell a joke, and be sure that you have the skill to do so, it must have relevance to what went before or what is to follow. In a business environment, where business is the object of your speech, you might be wise to avoid jokes altogether.

Proper use of humour is certainly essential and most great speakers have had the ability to use humour to develop a rapport with the audience. Churchill, Shaw and many others had an innate ability to insert humour into a serious topic and so make themselves more acceptable to audiences who possibly did not agree with their views. In the House of Commons today, Denis Skinner has the same ability to draw his listeners to him when his strong views on many subjects would normally make the same listeners walk away. It does, of course, go almost without saying that you should never tell jokes which might offend minority groups or even one member of your audience. Also avoid any jokes which might not be understood. Believe me, a dead joke is a dead speech, and rarely does an amateur comedian recognise his limitations.

Avoid clichés and make your presentation original

Of course you will include clichés since phrases which are really clichés come more readily to mind than any other, but if you want to be really successful try to eliminate them and put original thinking in their place.

Hold your audience by creating depth of emotion

If at all possible, get depth into your presentation by deliberately creating a few moments of real seriousness into your content. This can be done in a variety of ways, an example being a reference to the recent demise of a popular member of a club you are addressing. But however you do it, aim to bring the audience up in its tracks, just briefly, before you carry on with the speech you were presenting before. People like to have their emotions hit and your speech will certainly gain by achieving it.

Learn to recognise when you have exceeded your welcome

Always watch for the signs that you have gone on too long. These signs are self-evident in a babble of conversation which threatens to drown your own voice. They are evident in an audience looking around the room, at their watches, or even reading their dinner menus to see what they have just been served. If you cannot then re-arouse their interest by changing direction, it may well be time to cut short your speech and sit down. If you have overstayed your welcome, you will at least be given the benefit of having recognised it.

You cannot hold them all the time

If a distraction occurs, react to it and show that you are also human. A waiter who drops a tray of glasses will certainly get a response from the audience. Be quick enough to make a reaction yourself. A police siren past the window will also ensure that for a moment you have lost all contact with your listeners. Make sure you do not try and compete by trying to talk over it and pretending the distraction is not happening. By reacting in the same way as your audience you stand a better chance of relating to them and they to you. The only exception is a deliberate interruption from hecklers who may or may not have had too much alcohol for their own good. Beware of responding to that, since with this kind of 'internal' distraction you cannot win. Ignore it and leave its control to the organisers of the function where you are speaking.

The start and finish are all-important

Remember that in any speech, the most important parts must always be the initial opening and the conclusion. You can get away with a great deal if you create impact here and it is valuable to concentrate your most important points where they will best be remembered. Often this may mean that the initial opening is a menu outlining what you are going to say and your closing moments will be a summary of what you actually have said. Don't waste those opening minutes. 'Friends, Romans, Countrymen, lend me your ears' is a phrase recalled far swifter than anything in the speech which followed.

An encore may be demanded

If the topic is a well defined one and your speech can be short or long dependent on the reaction of the audience, always have available a 'buffer' or addition which you can use if you finish too early, if subsequent questions (assuming you welcome them) are not forthcoming or if your audience simply want an encore. The 'buffer' need not be long but it is advisable to avoid leaving your audience believing that they have been short-changed or that their demand for more has just been ignored. Any good singer or entertainer will have an encore available. As a speaker you should do the same, *but be sure that it is what the listeners really want.*

Clichés are for others, not the professional speaker

Finally, *never* finish with 'Thank you for your attention', 'Right, that's all I have to say', or 'I hope you are now as well informed on the subject as I'. These are all clichés which could have been written by any member of the audience and have no originality. Always aim to finish with a thought which sums up what you have said before and certainly with a phrase which your audience will remember. 'Give us the tools and we will finish the job' needed no further words added when it was originally said. It paraphrased the whole of the earlier speech, and was a phrase that was instantly memorable. I question whether it came to Winston Churchill without a great deal of thought and pre-planning.

Those are the basic rules for putting any good speech together, and I doubt whether you will go far wrong if you keep your framework within those guidelines. However, once you have outlined your talk, it is worthwhile checking through the framework to see whether the main points in it are evenly spaced or whether you need to introduce further examples or highlights which will bring your listeners back to you. This may mean moving your subject around so that interest is constantly maintained, since your speech will be remembered far more for the dull lifeless parts than for the areas which were packed with features and interest.

REHEARSING

The way you rehearse must necessarily be in a style with which you are comfortable. If you like to use a mirror or even a video camera, by all means do so, although my own belief is that it makes you far too self-conscious to concentrate adequately on the content of what you are saying. One way is to secure a friend who will sit in on your rehearsals and tell you honestly whether what you are doing is good or bad. This *can* work (or lose you a friend) but rarely is it used since we all believe that with practice we will recognise the faults and eliminate them for ourselves, and anyway we might well not get other than 'pretty good, yes, I liked it'.

What is probably going to be of much better value to you is to select a friend or colleague to sit in on your actual speech or talk and ask him specifically to note down criticisms, being as honest as he can, and then sit down with him afterwards to discuss his reaction. If he believes he is doing a worthwhile hatchet job for you then he will be far more likely to give positive and constructive criticism, rather than load you with compliments which are designed to give you what you want to hear. Certainly, you might make some errors in the first talk that he hears but you should certainly be better on the second and if he then asks you to give the same criticism to his own presentations, there should be some guarantee of honesty and constructive help in the advice that is offered.

Any speaker must be sincere, friendly, and approachable. Sincerity is presented by your enthusiasm and your own involvement in the subject. The authority that you stamp on your speaking comes, of course, from many factors, not least the content of what you say. It will, however, be increased by the emotion that you show and the confidence that you have in transmitting that emotion. Equally, sincerity can be destroyed by a lack of knowledge of the subject and even a failure to admit it when you are actually proved wrong.

The 'approachable' image, to ensure that the listener warms to *you*, often comes from an obvious informality and by ensuring that both you and your audience are relaxed in front of each other. It is generated by looking at the audience and by relaxing your own body movements so that your listener actually follows you. Unfortunately it is true that many speakers create a natural barrier between them and their listeners, and, however good the content of their material, find they cannot overcome the barrier to get their message across. That is why in charity appeals on television it has become the common practice to use for those appeals, not amateurs whose own enthusiasm and involvement in the appeal might never be in doubt, but actors who are professionally trained to reach out to the emotions of their audience.

In public speaking, as in no other use of the voice, a speaker is uncovering his own personality. He is opening up an area of himself. However, remember that whether your audience is five or five thousand, what you say and how you say it is merely an extension of a normal conversation between two people, the main difference being that one person remains the speaker and the other the listener. Remember this and you will go a long way to eliminating the self-consciousness which might otherwise take over.

CHECKLIST

- The larger audience presents problems of self-confidence.

- Learn the surroundings of where you are going to speak.

- Use notes as a guide, but *never* read your speech.

- Your audience will judge you by what they see as much as by what they hear.

- Work to a clear framework. The beginning and the end are all-important.

9

Improve your telephone technique

Well, if I called the wrong number, why did you answer the phone?

Cartoon caption in *The New Yorker*, 5 June 1937
(James Thurber, 1894–1961)

Constant telephone conversations and even telephone conferences now form a high percentage of the working day for many of us. Video telephones are still relatively rare and we must acknowledge that the use of the telephone as a method of communication still presents many differences compared with the advantages of face-to-face conversation. And yet, in most organisations, relatively little attention is given to training those who use the telephone to talk to customers, and little advice is given so that proper use is made of the advantages which the telephone offers.

ADVANTAGES AND DISADVANTAGES OF USING THE TELEPHONE

■ Initially you have far better access to a customer via the telephone than through almost any other method of contact. There will, of course, be those who consider that telephone rebuff is common but so is rebuff in almost any other approach. At least on the telephone, if you *are* rebuffed, you have wasted far less time than you would have done on a face-to-face approach. Small comfort maybe, but you do have the opportunity to call again, and possibly with more information than you had before. In addition, the listener, or recipient, will always regard a phone call as something of relatively limited duration and so more readily acceptable.

- On the telephone you have the opportunity to speak from an agenda, preparing it in advance of your conversation and ensuring that all the items you wished to discuss are included. They can then be marked off as they are dealt with, giving you the ability to be far more organised than you could in a face-to-face meeting where you may not even have the opportunity to refer to notes.

- If you present distractions in your dress or appearance, they will not be seen by the recipient of your call. Video telephones will change all this in time, but for the present you can be less careful about how you look and are less restricted by a timetable on when or how to make your call.

Against these advantages, you have disadvantages:

- You have no eye contact so are unable to convey warmth or sincerity with your body language. Your voice and your choice of words must do this instead, and this demands a far higher level of skill. In addition you have no assistance from brochures, samples or models and consequently need to rely on that vocal skill to convey the pictures and images that you could normally show directly. Surprisingly, your smile does get through, as can your posture, and by changing your posture you can convey a change of emphasis to your listener.

- If you are introducing yourself over the telephone, you do not have a visiting card or even a handshake as your initial opener. You need to make your own introduction, stating clearly who you are and the reason for your call. In general conversation this will often be a longer process, and a puzzled look on the face of the buyer or listener will often give you clear indication that your introduction has been inadequate and he is not really sure why you are there. On the telephone you have no such indicators and it is essential that this introduction is done formally, accurately, and right at the commencement of the call.

- You must be aware of the distractions which can present themselves in your own environment and eliminate them so that you concentrate solely on the call in hand. This means forgetting what is on the desk in front of you, ignoring distractions from others in the room, and certainly not taking your morning coffee while on the call. Believe me, if you only give 50 per cent attention to the call in hand, you will convey that impression very obviously down the line. A conscious effort is always necessary to ensure that your mind is totally on the telephone conversation in which you are involved.

SELECTING THE CORRECT APPROACH

The following set of rules will help guide your telephone manner:

The opener is all-important

Use your opening words skilfully. You have probably some 10–15 seconds, no more than, say, 30 words, to create an initial image of yourself from which you will be subsequently judged. You may be setting out your reasons for requesting an interview and those reasons must be immediately compelling. It is certainly worthwhile spending a disproportionate amount of time in getting those words right, since it will be from that opener that you will get the response you want. With a stranger, be immediately positive whilst you still have his attention. With a second call to the same person, you can afford to linger a little on the preliminaries since you have already made your introduction.

Ensure you give your name and purpose slowly

In any telephone call where you are making an initial approach, always ensure that you introduce yourself slowly. You may not get your listener to write your name down but at least he has the opportunity to do so if he wishes. You must aim to talk confidently and sound as if you are important enough to be considered important by the listener. Use names constantly and that means also finding out names. Ask and ask again until you know who you are speaking to, and then ensure you use that knowledge to get your message across. Remember that people like the personal approach and it is far too late to start asking for that information when your conversation is almost over.

Continually ask questions to secure information

Ask questions more often than you would in face-to-face discussion. In front of a customer you can often get acknowledgment of reaction from body language that you are being understood and how you are being received. On the telephone you have no such indications and asking positive questions is the only guide that you will get.

Listen rather than speak

Listen constantly to the recipient of your call and let him contribute. If your sole object is to say your piece, your one-way conversation will be just that. Two-way flow is as important on the telephone as it is in everyday conversation but is always that more difficult to achieve. The feedback that you get is all-important to ensure that you can alter your presentation to suit the listener. If you do not listen yourself, and that is the only feedback you have available, then you will miss out on analysing how good your presentation actually is.

In any communicating on the telephone, particularly on an incoming call, whether that call is an inquiry or even a complaint, always listen for as long as you can so that you can get the whole substance of the call before you decide on how you are going to deal with it. This is an important rule, particularly in selling, but it is even more important on the telephone where the time you each have available for a two-way conversation is usually limited.

Read between the lines

Since you do not have the advantage of visual aids to enable you to assess the reaction of the other person, look for hidden messages in his speech which will give you the indicators you are looking for. 'In my humble opinion' usually means exactly the opposite and shows that the speaker probably values his own views extremely highly. 'As you are aware' means he thinks that you are not really aware, or at the very least are not considering the point, and the speaker wishes to emphasise the matter so that you are more aware of it. 'Incidentally' often precedes the arrival of an important fact which is being made to look casual and of no consequence. 'Off the top of my head' means that he has probably worked out *exactly* what the price, date of delivery etc is going to be but in mentioning the price in that way he is sending out a trial signal to get a reaction, but has still left the situation open to later revise the price, or delivery date, or whatever. When you hear words like these, react by interpreting them as they should be interpreted, not as the speaker wants you to react. By listening for them you can gain a great deal of hidden meaning.

Record or make notes of what has been said

Use the advantage of not being seen to make notes of what is being said. It is far easier to review a telephone conversation afterwards if you have made rough notes as you went along. That means ensuring you always have paper and pen at your elbow. 'Just a minute, I'll get a pen' does little for your own credibility, and also holds up the process which you have just started. If you have to apologise for being unprofessional, that is just how your listener will remember you.

Prepare a plan before you speak

Again use the advantage of pre-planning to write down what you intend to say. You then have the ability to monitor what has been covered and what has yet to be discussed.

Aim to have a hook on which to hang your call

This means having a positive reason for making your call and a link so that you relate it to something which has occurred previously. This hook may be a letter you have written prior to your call, a new development you are promoting, or even a referral from a mutual friend, but it can be used effectively to make the call less unexpected and more readily received.

Leave the listener in no doubt why you are calling

Get to the point of your telephone call as swiftly as possible. It is very easy for the recipient of a call to make a positive decision to reject you, far easier than it is in a face-to-face meeting, and it is important that you get your initial subject across before a rejection decision is made. That does not necessarily mean asking for an order before you know acceptance is at least a probability, but it certainly means concentrating the first few seconds on gaining the right interest to carry on further.

Use references to others whenever you can

Use a referral whenever you can to establish a relationship, albeit through a third party, with your listener. A telephone conversation between two people who have never met and have never spoken before is inevitably a cold approach. The sooner you warm up that approach the better.

Remove other distractions from your mind

Never talk to anyone else, unless it is directly related to the call in hand, or permit anyone else to talk to you while you are on the telephone. Your job is to give you sole attention to the person you have phoned (or has phoned you) and it is bad manners to divert part of your interest to a separate unconnected matter.

Retain the initiative

If you are in a selling situation and the person you want is engaged, either wait until he is free, or leave a message that you have called and retain the initiative to re-make the call yourself. You should always avoid the temptation of accepting an offer from a colleague or a secretary that someone will ring you back. Not only have you lost control of the selling situation but, in addition, you have ensured that you need to be available while someone else chooses what time to ring you, and secondly you cannot make any further calls yourself until that one is out of the way.

Beware of contrived excuses for your call

Again, in a selling scenario, if that is the sole object of your call, do not try to mask it with stories of 'marketing', 'research' or other fabricated excuses for the real reason for your call. Let your listener know at the beginning that you are in the business of selling, and at the very least, if his reaction is going to be 'no', you have not wasted a great deal of time realising it.

Never leave your listener holding a dead telephone

Never keep someone waiting if there is likely to be a delay in securing the information that has been requested. If you need to search for a price list or for further information, advise that you will ring back shortly at a specific time if it is practical to do so, and then ring back *at that time*. The result will be a listener who will then be more receptive to what you have to say.

Check whether you have rung at an inconvenient time

Always check whether the recipient of your call is in a position to speak to you. When you phoned, he was almost certainly doing something else and if you give him the courtesy of deciding whether your call is more important than that, you have eliminated his possible determination to get back to what he was doing as swiftly as possible. In a face-to-face conversation, you can see when is the right moment to break in, but on the phone you have no knowledge of what the recipient is doing when your call arrives. By asking his permission to interrupt, you secure a decision in your own favour (an agreement to talk to you), and your professionalism will be recognised and appreciated. If, on the other hand, the response that you get tells you that you have broken in at the wrong time, then make your call again at a more favourable time when you have a willing listener rather than a reluctant one.

Match your style to the listener

Try to make your responses in the same vein as the questions you get. Someone who makes those requests in a brisk efficient way will usually welcome the reply in the same style while a slower thinker (and probably speaker) will indicate by his own manner the speed at which he would prefer the conversation to move. Remember that however you normally speak, you must always take your cue from the other person.

A contrived break sometimes helps

If you find yourself in a situation where you need time to think, make an excuse, and then use the opportunity to restart. It may seem contrived, but just placing your finger on the hook of the telephone, so cutting off the conversation, can sometimes give you the space you need to restart with a different approach when you reconnect. Sometimes if the conversation seems to be slipping out of control you *need* a break to gather your thoughts (or even get a swift word of advice from a colleague). Use the tactic sparingly but be aware that it is there.

Never take a call you cannot properly handle

This sometimes means leaving a telephone ringing if you are otherwise engaged and cannot deal with it in the proper way, either by speaking to the caller or transferring the call to someone else. This may be bad selling to leave the phone ringing, but it is certainly better than picking it up and then explaining that you are already engaged and that you need to place the caller on hold.

Leave the door open

Whatever reaction you get from your prospect, remember that he or she might still be a prospect at a later date and you should never shut the door on a further approach in the future. Prospects are the life-blood of your business and it is foolish to lose them permanently simply because they cannot be converted at that particular time.

CONCLUSION

Finally, when using the telephone, never underestimate its value as a method of communication which gives more immediate access to other people than any other method at your disposal. Used correctly and positively it is an enormous asset to any business but it is unfortunately regarded often as a second-rate style of communication which needs little or no formal training to be effective. When telephoning, some people are not able to retain the same relaxed approach they may well have when dealing with people face-to-face, and find more difficulty in being effective when they cannot see the person they are talking to. The lack of visual advantages means that far more attention to words, vocabulary and method of presentation must be given than you ever need in everyday conversation. For all that, the results in business can be so immediate that the training you give yourself, and indeed your staff, is more than repaid by those results. Ignore that training and you will be wasting one of the finest worktools at your disposal.

CHECKLIST

- Be aware of the advantages and disadvantages of telephone selling.

- Be prepared to listen rather than speak.

- Keep a written record of what has been said.

- Prepare your presentation beforehand so nothing important is omitted.

- Ensure your listener is receptive and is open to your call.

10

Translating good speech into good writing

What is written without effort is generally read without pleasure.

Dr Samuel Johnson (1709–1784)

I f you do not communicate by speaking, then you probably do so by writing. Often, in business anyway, someone who speaks effectively and persuasively is unable to get the same message across when he is writing, either to his customers or to his staff. There are many reasons why the two methods of presentation need a different approach, the principal two being as follows:

1. The main difference is that in writing, you need to concentrate more on being correct since you only have one chance to make the presentation, and, more important, you will not be there when it is read so you are unable to vary the contents as it is presented. In addition, you do not have the advantage of your own visual impact, your gestures and your persuasive ability. As a result, the choice of words that you use assumes a far greater importance.

2. The advantage of writing is that, in addition to your being able to re-read and review it yourself, your reader can do the same, so even if it proves a little difficult for him to understand initially, it can be read and re-read by the recipient in his own time, which means he can give it his undivided attention when other matters are not on his mind. If a reader is distracted, he can merely go back to try to absorb it a second time. In face-to-face communication listeners have only one chance of understanding what is said, then that moment has gone.

THE FEATURES OF GOOD AND PERSUASIVE WRITING

What features must you put into your writing to ensure that the result is as persuasive as your own speaking and what differences between speaking and writing should you be aware of? One skill is not easier or more difficult than the other, but each certainly presents different demands.

As with speaking, the art of writing is neither acquired overnight nor by reading one chapter from a book, even this one. However, having said that, while there may be many who are gifted and will write (or speak) more naturally than others, writing is a skill which can be learnt as any other. This is done largely by working at it and practising one's own skills, but also by reading the styles and standards of others, recognising good English when you see it, and then transferring that style to your own.

The problem is that most people who are aware that their style is poor generally feel unable to improve or to alter the clarity and impact of their writing. They may not even be aware whether their style is good or bad, even if they are aware that others seem to express themselves with more confidence than they do themselves, but they may have little idea where to secure the right guidelines. One has only to glance in the correspondence columns of the local newspapers to see how ineffective some of those letters are, in spite of the fact that the opinions were set down by people with strong emotions on the subject they were writing about. And, regardless of the fact that all those letters were probably honed and rewritten a dozen times before being submitted, the final effect often proves difficult to read, the real meaning sometimes impossible to understand, and the impact that they wanted to convey never reaches the reader at all.

A revision of the basics of grammar is not necessary

The rules of grammar are, of course, more than could be contained in this chapter, or indeed in this book. However, I doubt whether there are many who would be prepared to sit down and repeat the studying of grammar which most of us have already suffered at school. Grammar is a complex topic and it is necessarily a long time before a good workable knowledge of it has any great effect on our own writing. We should, however, be at least aware of the way in which the basic words that we use are divided up so that we can talk more sensibly about the kind of words that we should use and when we should use them.

Writing style can be divided into:

- the length of the paragraphs to indicate the framework;
- the length of the sentences to divide the separate thoughts;
- the selection of nouns to convey the initial picture;
- the selection of verbs to clarify your specific meaning;
- the selection of adjectives to colour the image for the reader;
- the choice of pronouns demanded by our personal approach to the reader.

Paragraphs separate one topic from the next

The length of a paragraph *in itself* is not greatly important. What is important is what it contains and whether it contains too many ideas. Paragraphs should indicate a simple framework and one which is not daunting for the reader. A long, convoluted paragraph containing a large number of different topics is difficult to digest, and, if it is also difficult to read, will neither be read nor absorbed. The rule of matching one paragraph to one idea should rarely be broken, since that is the reason for the break at the end of it, namely to give a physical pause before the next idea is presented.

Sentences are smaller ideas within the paragraph

The sentences within that paragraph should also be limited to one thought for each, again restricting the length so that the meaning is obvious and is not complicated by changing the direction of thought in the middle. The length of sentences has, over the last sixty years, become a great deal shorter. If you read the works of a writer from the 1930s you will find that sentences of 30 words or more were common. Nowadays under 20 words would be considered more reasonable. Certainly people's ability to read has probably diminished over the same time but, even taking that into account, it has become well recognised that long sentences (and long paragraphs) make hard work for the reader. That is what you should be aiming to avoid. The length of sentences is ce   nly a matter of custom and the personality of the writer, but the need to make the listener understand as easily as possible is a vital skill of the writer who is also aiming to sell. Aim to make as many short sentences as you can, while still ensuring that the length of them varies enough to avoid monotony.

A wide range of choice in your nouns is essential

Initially, the noun is probably the most pictorial word that we are able to use and, depending on our choice, will give the best initial image of what we are trying to convey. The positive or concrete nouns such as *house* or *cottage* or *dwelling* all convey, in different forms depending on our own experiences, a picture. Here the actual choice of words, and fairly similar words at that, is vitally important since the conventional image can be formed without any further description. Obviously the more of those words that you have at your disposal, the more specific each can be, and the less demanding the additional words need be to colour them further. Abstract nouns such as 'pleasure' cannot be visualised at all but positive and concrete nouns should be as easy to picture as possible. The specific aim of a noun must be to give clarity and image to your writing, and the advice in an earlier chapter to increase the vocabulary that you have available is the best way of ensuring that.

Verbs present the most likely area for mistakes

The verb is less important to spend time on to a certain extent, since we probably all have a wide command of verbs. It is difficult to express ourselves at all without a very specific verb to describe exactly what we mean. However, verbs have many variants of future, past and present tense (and others) and it is in this grammatical application that the average person makes his mistakes. 'I were coming along the road.' 'You was due to telephone me yesterday.' Both types of remark are heard every day and yet their correction is ignored even though the speaker must be aware, from listening to the majority of others, that an error has been made. It is probably not important at all if the conveyance of meaning is the only reason for speaking in the first place, but if we wish to speak with conviction, we must eliminate as many of those errors as possible from our repertoire. However, while correct use of verbs is important for the imagery and the picture you create, they are less critical than the proper choice of other words such as nouns and adjectives.

Get your imagery from the right choice of adjectives

Perhaps even more than the noun, the adjective creates images (or fails to do so if the wrong one is used). When you are speaking, the use of inadequate adjectives can sometimes be overcome by a more expressive way of saying them. 'It was a huge house' says something different from 'it was a *huge* house', but in writing, the use of the same adjective can only be interpreted in one way by the reader. 'I went to a nice party' says nothing. 'I went to an uproarious party' at least conveys some image of the kind of occasion that it was. Yet for all that, I expect that on almost every holiday postcard sent back from Majorca, Blackpool or wherever, the word 'nice' appears at least once. Add a further adjective if you want, and say 'I went to an uproarious fancy-dress (used as an adjective) party' and the picture is enhanced yet again. Many people with little imagination will use that same word 'nice' to describe two completely different occasions. It is not that we do not know alternative words since few of us are that limited, but we do not consider, in our writing, whether the word that we are actually using is the right one to convey the maximum effect.

Adverbs are really adjectives also, except they qualify a verb rather than a noun. Again, to use similar examples, you could say 'He ran nicely', or 'he ran gracefully', or 'powerfully'. The first example adds nothing to the meaning, while the alternatives add colour to what you are trying to say.

Pronouns are the easiest words to misuse

What about pronouns and the way they relate to what has been said before? Here the most common errors are made, even by skilled writers who should know better. Pronouns must relate to something, and if the noun they should relate to is not clear, then it is as well to change the construction of the whole sentence so that it *is* clear. Every day, in the newspapers, we read reports like 'The judge told the defendant that he had a problem.' Confusion has been created since, without knowing the circumstances, we do not know who had the problem – the judge or the defendant. A simple alteration such as 'The judge, in his summing up, said that the defendant had a problem' removes that confusion and removes also the need for the listener to work it out for himself.

The only gauge as to whether the use of a pronoun is correct or incorrect is to substitute it for the noun it relates to. For instance, consider the statement 'A person who throws litter out of a car is a litter lout. They should be prosecuted.' 'They' refers to no one mentioned earlier. The simple solution is either to alter 'A person' in the first sentence to 'people' or 'They' to 'He' in the second sentence. So far as the meaning is concerned, few people would be confused, but while the first usage is discordant, the second becomes acceptable. Many people will not even recognise the error but, if you are aiming to make your own presentation as correct as possible, you must be constantly aware of the link between words in consecutive or related sentences.

There are, of course, certain nouns where that rule is not so clear cut, as for example in 'The audience applauded' (did it or did they?). In cases like that you need to decide for yourself whether the appropriate pronoun to follow will be singular or plural. You merely have to read it and if both opinions sound equally right, then either will probably be equally acceptable to the listener.

Persuasive writing demands colourful words

Without going any further into the rules of grammar here, it is obvious that the imagery that we create is probably our most important consideration so that we convey in our writing the same colour that we aim to convey in our speaking. This is not purely the imagery of fiction, although that is a skill belonging to even fewer writers, but it is the ability to show in our writing, our social letters, and certainly in our business letters, that we mean what we say and convey the image that is in our own minds with as little effort as possible being demanded from our reader.

The actual order of words is the syntax, it is the style, it is the usage. It is the law which advises you not to split an infinitive; 'to hurriedly go' instead of 'to go hurriedly', although this particular rule can probably be broken more often than most. What is important is that you cultivate, from reading the works of others, a feeling for what sounds correct and what grates so that you can avoid the same errors yourself. In the end, obeying as many of the rules of syntax and grammar as you can, it is far more important that the meaning is logical and clear rather than adhering to a set series of rules. A misplaced word *can* alter the meaning. Advertisements such as 'Piano wanted by lady with carved legs' are not unusual and are written in that way simply because the writer cannot take the trouble to read it back to himself or herself before deciding whether it is right.

The various specific rules of grammar such as placing adverb after a verb, or not splitting infinitives are only really valid if the result sounds incorrect or lumbering. If, on rereading, it sounds equally correct either way, then make the choice subjective and use whichever version you prefer. Rules of grammar are made to be acceptable to the speaker, the reader and the listener, and phrases can sound far more artificial if you are forcing the words into a format where they obey the rules of grammar but still sound incorrect. For instance, 'to clearly understand the subject' with the emphasis on 'clearly', is equally rhythmical as 'to understand the subject clearly', and yet there will be many who will condemn the former simply because it breaks a simple rule of grammar.

In some languages the order of words is all important, possibly French and certainly Latin, but English has a far more flexible set of rules and your writing has a far more natural rhythm if you are prepared to juggle with the words until they sound right.

Ineffective writing is careless writing

The majority of us can certainly write. Some may even believe they can write well, yet still be doing it badly, while others may know their writing is inadequate and not have the will to do anything positive about it. For those of you who *do* want to improve and who believe that you can gain socially and in business from doing so, there are many areas where a proper preparation of your ideas, and indeed a proper edit of your finished work, can result in a far more effective result than you are achieving now.

As already mentioned, a complete relearning of English grammar is unnecessary. You need only familiarise yourself with a few basic rules. What is far more important in your writing is to produce something which sounds correct and does not jar. Good English changes all the time and different writers will express the same thought in a totally different way, one using one style and one another. What you must do is to cultivate the skill of recognising bad or clumsy style when you see it so that when you see the same in your own writing, you can change it to something which is more acceptable to read. That, after all, is the real advantage of writing against speaking. The only way you will recognise good English in your own writing or in that of others is to read constantly and observantly.

ACQUIRING A NEW WRITTEN STYLE

Reading observantly means reading slowly, or, even better, reading out loud. A sentence which has been written without a subject, or a proper verb, or an ending should then immediately stand out in a way that it will not do if the work is simply skimmed. You need to look for the construction of the meaning in the same way that at school you recognised that 'The cat sat on the mat' formed a simple positive statement which meant something. All sentences must have that skeleton and, if your sentences are kept short, the skeleton can be easily isolated. Having recognised that skeleton, you are able to add the descriptive adjectives to describe the cat and the mat, and follow that with the adverbs to qualify the sitting, all of which then colour the main sentence. It is because many people fail to start with a framework, even to a simple sentence, or make their sentences so long that the framework disappears altogether, that the final result is not as clear and concise as they had planned. The following set of rules is designed to help you write more clearly and effectively.

Start with a summary of why you are writing

Always, in any correspondence, summarise what might have taken place previously, whether that was a meeting or an earlier letter, and lead through to the reason why the new letter is being written at all. Then say whatever is new, keeping to as many of the following rules as possible. Finally, summarise what you have said, the reasons for saying it, and where you expect the action to go from then on.

Simplicity in construction is clarity for the reader

Keep your paragraphs and sentences short so that you, and the reader, can see the framework. Write longer and more complicated sentences only when you are confident that you can do so without losing the thread of your argument.

Use imagery to convey your picture

When you have established the basic sentence, colour it as you would a picture, listing all the descriptive words you have to hand, and choosing the one which best conveys what you visualise. Colourful language is not difficult but it does require more effort to describe a car as 'Sunset Red' than merely 'Red' and that is why advertising copy-writers in the motor industry are paid good money to find better words to build a picture in the minds of their prospective buyers. 'Tingling Fresh' really does not say a great deal more than 'Fresh' but it *does* help the listener or reader on his way if he is trying to create an image of what is being said.

Take time to select the right words

The choice of words is no less important in writing than it is in speaking but in writing you have the time to balance the value of one word against another and decide which of those available is the best choice. Even the use of a dictionary or a thesaurus will help those whose imagination cannot conjure up a worthwhile selection from which to choose. The problem is that most people write so quickly, or are so reluctant to review their work, that the first thought which goes down is probably the one which stays on the paper. If what you create does *not* present a picture, then you are making hard work for your reader who then needs to do that work for himself.

Similes provide instant pictures

Continuing on the same theme, the use of pictorial language covers the use of metaphors, similes and comparative phrases which are all ways of providing a different image to the listener (or reader). Metaphors such as 'All hands to the wheel' give an instant picture of people cooperating to get a job done. Another example would be to describe a tourist as 'Bristling with cameras', a description which says the same as 'having many cameras round his neck' but says it in a way which instantly recalls for the listener a memory of something which he has seen somewhere else in the past. A simile is almost identical to a metaphor but usually provides a comparison with something more pictorial and will invariably include the word 'like'. 'Walking through the snow was like wading through a pile of cotton wool.' 'The atmo-sphere was like Aberdeen on a wet Sunday.' 'Talking to him was like conversing with a plastic bucket.' In all these examples, phrases are used which are designed to create imagery, to convert abstract ideas to recognisable pictures, and arouse the imagination of someone needing to picture the scene.

Make your writing style conversational

Write so that your language is informal and conversational. That does not mean ungrammatical but it certainly means leaning towards a style which you would expect to hear in everyday talk. Writing once demanded a special style of its own and many recognised authors of the 1920s and 1930s sound stilted when they are read today. We have become far less constricted by set standards and we can now break the established rules more often if we feel that our writing sounds better by doing so. Splitting infinitives and ending sentences with prepositions were once rules that authors broke at their peril. In modern writing, the result will often sound artificial if you keep to such rules. Again, compare your own work with that of others and see whether your style sounds stilted or not. Take care, however, when using colloquialisms and slang. This demands a more skilful approach and care is needed if such usage is not to sound as contrived as the formal style you are trying to avoid.

Monitor and correct your spelling

If you have a problem with spelling, the only real way to improve is to read and recognise correct spelling in others. A misspelt word in a page of writing stands out and immediately creates the wrong image about the writer. Those who say that poor spelling is of little consequence are generally those who cannot take the trouble to correct their own errors. Remember that the words you misspell are probably few and are certainly out of proportion to the negative opinion that they create.

Develop the skilful use of punctuation

Use pauses as you do in speaking. This comes back to short sentences, but it also includes the use of commas and breaks in your writing to help the reader maintain the same rhythm as you created when you wrote it. Put it on paper without those breaks and you will not only create uncertainty in your reader, who is not sure where one thought stops and another starts, but you will give no idea of the rhythm in which it was originally written.

In the past the rules of punctuation have always been a little too rigid, particularly in the restriction of where one type of punctuation can be used and where another cannot. The easiest rule of all is to use commas throughout to provide the short hesitations and breaks, sometimes to create a pause and sometimes to introduce a separate phrase in the middle of another. Use full stops to herald a new idea or where you wish to indicate a more definite break. Then, having placed your punctuation where you think it should be, read your work out loud. If any pause which has been created appears to be inadequate, strengthen it by making a comma into a semicolon or even into a full stop. If the comma appears too short, it can even be extended into a dash, and if the comma does not bring the sense to as firm a conclusion as you would like, that may well be the place to insert a full stop and start a new sentence. The whole object of punctuation is to break the sense as you would in conversation, and if it fails to do so, then it needs to be altered even if that seems to go against the set rules that the grammar book advises. That may mean making sentences shorter (or longer), but either way, reading out loud should tell you whether your work has been punctuated correctly or not and whether it conveys the impression you are aiming for. If spoken conversation does not demand a pause, then generally neither should your writing.

Lastly, never overdo punctuation. Forget multiple exclamation or question marks which are merely an excuse for not having expressed your views more strongly. Amateurs rely on punctuation, particularly the exclamation mark or question mark, to hammer home a point when a proper choice of words would have done exactly the same but with more style. A single exclamation mark indicates to the reader that you expect him to be surprised, and in that context is not only acceptable but probably good writing also. Excessive punctuation is for the writers of comics. In professional writing, the punctuation will not even be noticed.

Plan your writing within a framework

Always gather your thoughts into a preconceived plan and not one which occurs to you as you go along. There are writers whose ideas are so prolific that their writing just flows but rarely are they able to find that same ability in the reader whose skills at following the thread might be more limited. Consequently the structure that the reader is looking for is either not there or is difficult to find. Work to a plan which both you and the reader can recognise and you will then be in a format which the other can relate to.

Avoid the regular use of clichés

Whatever you write, make it original. This means avoiding the excessive use of clichés and the words which other people expect you to say. Giles, in his cartoons, always calls a fête a 'Grand' fête simply because that is what people with no imagination always call it. Yet in spite of the humour the word engenders, the words 'Grand Fête' still occur regularly in every village in England throughout the summer. If a word is overused, if it is a cliché, then discard it and choose another more descriptive one – one just as pictorial, but at least one of your own. Use of the predictable words sounds trite and results also in a reader who will skim through what you have written rather than read it with enthusiasm. Aim to arouse your reader with a word or phrase he was not expecting. Consider the impact of those words of Brian Hanrahan in the Falklands War. 'I counted them out and I counted them back.' Originality and effect in one short sentence. Avoid slang, because those words are usually clichés anyway. Make your work original.

Space your strong points evenly throughout your work

When constructing an argument or a proposal in any piece of writing, build that argument gradually but ensure that the strong points are well covered throughout. If you leave them all to the end (as a conclusion), your reader might not get that far, while if you list them all at the beginning, your reader might dismiss the following arguments supporting them. Whether the subject on which you are writing needs three pages or 300, make sure that you give each page a degree of importance. If that is difficult, then maybe there should be fewer pages.

Revise and review until it is right

Always make use of your ability to rewrite and to review. It is a good idea to reread it the next day, before preparing your final draft. An angry letter in particular will usually gain by revision, often by making it sound less angry and therefore more effective, while a sales letter may gain by possibly raising another benefit you had not listed previously.

A long letter can often secure more impact by being made shorter. A too short letter can be made more effective by elaborating points which appear unclear, while a comma might have been left out or one too many put in. Certainly a revision before a letter is published or sent can often uncover errors which were not evident earlier, and rarely are any of us that skilled that we get it 100 per cent right the first time. The ability to revise is a valuable advantage and if you throw that advantage away because you are short of time, you bring your writing down to the level of the impromptu scribble. Even though it will take up more of your time, never regard your first draft as your final copy. In the words of Blaise Pascal who wrote in 1640, 'I have made this letter longer than usual, only because I have not had the time to make it shorter'. Letter writing and good composition take effort and you will rarely achieve a successful result the first time round.

There must always be more to your writing than keeping to the rules of grammar and vocabulary since the whole object of creative and assertive writing is to secure interest, to convince, and indeed to make the reader wish to carry on reading. Each paragraph should have a compelling interest that encourages the reader to expect the same interest from the next paragraph. Remember that it is easier for a reader to stop reading than it is for a listener to stop listening. If you write in a dull manner you make that decision easier still.

Writing for business or pleasure is one of the most satisfying skills. Unlike conversation, you have a permanent record of what you have done. The ability to write well and influence others by writing well, will place you amongst the minority of those who take as much (or more) trouble with their writing as they do with their conversation, and the improvement of those skills will give you a leading edge you might not have had before. The writers of good business letters are rare – make sure you are one of them.

CHECKLIST

- Good writing means holding the reader's attention until he has finished.

- An ability to choose from a wide range of words is paramount.

- The effective use of imagery will put colour into your writing.

- Learn the basic rules of good writing and the use of punctuation.

- Paragraphs and sentences must fall easily into an overall framework.

- Reading the good writing of others will encourage your own style.

- Revision and review will always improve what you have written.

11

Avoiding the most common mistakes

All the great speakers were bad speakers at first.

Ralph Waldo Emerson (1803–1882)

This chapter brings you back to both reading and writing since, while I have emphasised that the skills required in the two are different, and indeed they are, the same set of rules to 'get it right' can be applied in many situations.

Probably the most common mistake of all is ignoring the requirements of the listener or the reader. This means avoiding making your own performance the main element in your speaking but concentrating the whole time on placing yourself at the receiving end, and moreover doing it in a way that tries to understand the listener's own capabilities. If, as a BBC commentator, you are describing a game of snooker, to get 100 per cent acceptance you must consider the one person who has a black and white TV set. You might well consider the 99.5 per cent acceptance is good enough, but there will be other, similar, comparisons where you may not get through to 50 per cent or even more of your audience. Politicians are remarkably bad at assessing their audience, and I would question whether, on budget day, the Chancellor is speaking to more than about 25 per cent of his listeners. There *are* ways of increasing your audience participation, and these will be discussed in this chapter.

TELL YOUR LISTENERS WHAT THEY WANT TO HEAR

Firstly, consider what your listener actually wants. He comes to be entertained, or to be informed, or possibly even stimulated. However, his receptiveness and concentration will be broken down by numerous different distractions over which you may or may not have control. If, in a public speech, those distractions come from a pneumatic drill outside, then maybe you have to live with it and counter by raising your voice. The distractions you create yourself, however, can be avoided.

Create visual impact

Your own appearance must, of course, be neutral, not untidy, and certainly not over-decorative. The bow tie you think is absolutely magnificent might just distract the audience you are trying to convince.

Use volume to be heard – not to dominate

Your voice must be at a level which can be heard but never at a level which annoys. The Rev. Ian Paisley always appears to be trying to shout down the opposition. There will, of course, be occasions when a raised voice will lend drama and conviction to what you are saying, but if that is your standard volume level, then for emphasis you have nowhere else to go.

Avoid repetition

Avoid making excessive use of a particular word or phrase. Do so and your audience will soon be waiting for it to the detriment of what they should be listening to.

Vary your speed to create interest

Avoid the 'metronome' effect. Boring speakers are rarely aware that a small variation in their production and an effort in changing their style and use of words could dramatically alter their impact (and their own popularity).

Keep body movements neutral

Do not infuriate the listeners with over-exaggerated hand signals. Hand gestures are useful when they are used in moderation but any good speaker would be wise to concentrate much more on letting his arms rest in a neutral position by the side of the body.

THE ERRORS WHICH ANNOY

What annoys others most in conversation? While you are seeking to achieve star qualities, what should you avoid if you are to be a real success? My own list of errors and suggestions both for social and business conversation would certainly include the following:

Speak of what you know: Probably the most common error in any conversation, whether it be business or social, is to be ignorant of the subject under discussion, yet human nature being what it is, rarely are we prepared to admit that the views of another might have more basis or relevance. We should always be prepared to recognise when the opinions of others might have precedence over our own.

Interruption is bad communication and is also discourteous: Avoid breaking in on someone before he has finished speaking and always think twice before you have decided he has finished. The error of anticipating the end of someone else's conversation, either by supplying the end yourself, or worse, supplying a contradictory view, is probably one of the most unacceptable barriers to creating any flow in conversation. It implies arrogance and a picture of someone whose sole object is to express his own view and not be prepared to listen also to the views of others. People often *do* finish the sentences of others, essentially because they know what that person is going to say and want to indicate that fact, but also so that they can then take control of the conversation.

A raised voice indicates lack of control: Never believe that added conviction can be achieved by raising your voice. There are certain occasions where for various reasons an adjustment in pitch is called for, but a voice which is raised as the result of strong emotions will usually have the result of making what is said of less importance, for two reasons. Firstly, because your words will no longer be as easily understood and secondly, because you will raise the hackles of your listener who will then be less receptive to what you have to say. In addition, if you are talking to one or two people in a room where the room is also full of others, a raised voice is particularly irritating since it intrudes on the conversations of others. Many people, either through nervousness or ignorance, and sometimes even through brashness, speak too loudly, but you can be sure that it will usually be interpreted as loud-mouthed or arrogant by others.

Concentrate on your skills as a listener: Always concentrate on looking like a listener who has interest in others and their views. This means listening with your eyes and your body language. Mistakes in this field include obvious distractions such as looking elsewhere, manicuring your finger nails or letting your mind wander elsewhere and making that evident. A bad listener will swiftly be rejected by others who also want to put forward their point of view but will not do so to someone who is patently not listening.

Bring colour and life into your voice: Avoid any presentation which has no colour and no rhythm. Rarely will you be told you are falling into this error, and it is probably one of the most difficult to discover for yourself. The use of a tape recorder will help you to hear yourself as others hear you and it is certainly true that in your normal everyday speech, what you hear as a speaker in no way represents what your listener also hears. Decide whether *you* would accept that type of pitch or presentation from others speaking to you and, if not, analyse what needs to be changed. Many accept the principle of using tape recording to analyse their performance but few actually do it and fewer still have friends who are honest enough to give the right criticism so that errors can be eliminated.

It is not difficult to alter your pitch and style. What *is* difficult is recognising that it needs to be altered at all. A monotonous voice sounds bored, whether that is the real truth or not. Albeit unfairly, people judge a speaker from the way he sounds before they judge him by what he actually says.

Match your presentation to that of your listener: Always aim to run the pace of your conversation to suit your listener. People *do* have a range of speeds that their minds can accept and if you speak outside that range you will be interpreted as someone who appears to be talking above his audience. Sometimes, of course, someone talking to you may be projecting outside your own range and, if possible, an adjustment of your own capability as a listener might be called for.

Swearing is for parrots: Avoid bad language. Your listener will rarely react except in his own private reaction to you. Use of bad language indicates a lack of depth in the vocabulary you have available: it has no place in business or social conversation and demeans the person who uses it. If you feel strong language is necessary to emphasise a point, then you need to extend your vocabulary to include more colourful and less offensive words.

Listen to others and adopt their ways: Work at avoiding the misuse of words and bad grammar by listening (and reading) those who should get it right (newscasters usually do), and if you find that it is not the way you do it yourself, take the trouble to find out who is wrong. In your own conversation you are probably not making many obvious mistakes but the ones you *are* making are probably being made too often and mark you as a person whose education is letting you down. Regular mistakes will damage your image and credibility, particularly if they are mistakes which, with a little effort, could be eliminated.

Be prepared to compromise: Avoid entering into any conversation or discussion with your views and opinions already fixed. It is essential that you gear your mind to consider the other point of view, even if, at the end of it, you fail to be convinced. Remember that your own view is worth little if you haven't at some time considered it against the views of others. In your responses in any conversation, always acknowledge those views before putting forward your own. Even if you do not agree, you should show empathy for another whose views are probably as strongly held as your own. Compromise is, after all, the basis of any relationship with another, and good conversation thrives on that fact.

Whether you agree or not, always respect another person's opinions.

Develop the art of patience: Always aim to have patience, both as a speaker and as a listener. Many conversations break down or are ineffective simply because one person does not have patience with another and becomes irritated if he seems unable to get his views across.

The more common mistakes can be avoided but only if you are prepared to do something about it. Most people who have no real need of conversation in their business lives, and who move in social circles where poor expression is the norm, can usually get away with lower standards than they might otherwise need. If you fall into that category, fine. But, from the fact that you are reading this book at all, I would assume that you recognise the importance of getting the best out of the communication skills that you have, and recognise also that, with a little effort, it is possible to raise those standards so that you achieve something better. Avoid the mistakes listed above and you will be well on your way.

CHECKLIST

- Know what your listener is expecting to hear.

- Be aware of the distractions you create by your own behaviour.

- Learn to become a skilful listener.

- Always be prepared to compromise or to be convinced by others.

- Improvement is usually achieved by adopting the good styles of others.

12

Be more confident!

The great pleasure in life is doing what people say you cannot do.

Walter Bagehot (1826–1897)

The main problem, of course, is that even by reading this or any other book, you cannot immediately become an effective and convincing speaker. What will take you in that direction is constant practice. It is the knowledge that you are above to avoid the stumbling blocks which cause nervousness and the knowledge that failure can be avoided which will gradually build the self-confidence you need to get it right every time.

You need to practise, to yourself and indeed to outside audiences, to secure the self-confidence which tells you you will not dry up, that your listeners will appreciate what you have to say and will indeed look forward to listening to you. To speak and write with conviction, you need confidence in yourself and your own ability. This means being at ease with other people and having the knowledge that you can talk to them on even terms. It means being able to express yourself forcefully and concisely in a way which matches both the occasion and the listener. It means being prepared to choose your words and how you say them, knowing what is right and wrong and being able to correct the mistakes that you make.

TRAIN YOURSELF

There are public speaking clubs and meetings where you are able to practise in front of others whose criticism will help in setting you along the right path. Debating societies as training grounds are certainly one

of the most effective ways of getting the kind of self-confidence that
you need. They will:

- give you a chance of planning a speech or talk, and often to a length
  which you can determine yourself;

- give you the discipline to research a topic and select arguments
  which suit your own style and are relevant to your audience;

- encourage you to project your ideas among people who will be
  prepared to criticise you and give you constructive advice on ways
  of improving your presentation. This criticism will be constructive
  since they will be looking for the same approach from yourself;

- encourage you to develop enthusiasm for a subject for which
  initially you may have no enthusiasm at all. Call it play-acting if
  you wish, but very often you need to give a subject a priority which
  you know your audience supports but which on the surface you
  may not share yourself;

- train you in the art of persuasion so that you gain confidence in
  your ability to sway others to your point of view.

THE BASIC RULES

There are, of course, many guidelines which will give you the confidence you are seeking, but a few basic rules are mandatory:

1. *You must be knowledgeable*
   You must know your subject and have valid reason for saying, and
   backing, your opinions and views. To talk about subjects of which
   you patently know little is to ensure that your listeners will not
   take you seriously, and will damage your own self-confidence
   before you start.

2. *You must listen*
   You must develop the skill, and that is just what it is, of listening to
   the opinions of others and analysing what they want to hear from
   you. For your conversation to be effective, you must have a
   receptive audience – not an audience who necessarily agrees with
   you but one which certainly is prepared to absorb and consider
   your point of view. If you tread on territory where you should not
   be, you will swiftly lose your listener who will decide you do not
   have the authority to talk on that subject at all.

3. *You must be in control*
   If your conversation is in a business setting, you must, if possible, control the pace and decide when you switch from stating the problem to the point where you search for the solution. This may not be your formal responsibility as chairperson or whatever, but it is certainly an area in which you as a participant can make a proper contribution.

4. *Review often what has gone before*
   If you reach the point where you need to make an assertion (or a decision) then ensure you summarise what has gone before. If speaking effectively and with conviction means convincing others, you will often need to reaffirm the path you took in reaching your conclusion.

5. *Eliminate the abrasives*
   You need to practise all the time to eliminate from your own conversation the mannerisms and phrases which annoy others. There are many phrases we use which deliberately set out to annoy and indicate that our own opinions are infallible. 'I cannot believe that you really think that' is a typical example. Avoid creating barriers when what you should be doing is trying to remove them.

6. *Think positively that nothing will go wrong*
   Remember that nervousness is the fear of something that *might* happen and that nervousness will go if you can eliminate that particular fear. This means being conscious that you have acquired or improved an ability to communicate effectively with others.

WHAT ARE YOU AFRAID OF?

You may be afraid for any one of a number of reasons:

- You feel that your audience will reject you. Analyse why. If it is the subject, then prepare it more skilfully so that you are confident of your own knowledge.

- You believe that your listeners will lose attention, and their minds (or themselves) will drift off elsewhere. Improve your presentation so that your enthusiasm will carry others.

■ You think you will dry up and lose track of what you have to say. This can only happen if you have prepared inadequately. The solution to this lies in your own hands.

■ People may not laugh at your jokes. Either accept your limitations and do not tell jokes or alternatively develop a better technique. A failed joke causes embarrassment while a joke aimed at the wrong audience can easily become a failed joke. Unless you are totally proficient in storytelling, tread warily. Humour is easy and relaxing but jokes need more careful handling. Rarely will others tell you that you are doing it wrong.

■ Nervousness may be inevitable. If you are making a business presentation, a bad speech might affect your chances of promotion or even continued employment. That can certainly happen and would create apprehension in anyone. However, there *are* ways of ensuring that you don't make a bad speech and speakers rarely take all the steps needed to ensure they have avoided as many risks as possible. It may not be possible to eliminate nervousness altogether (that might not be a good target anyway) but at least you can feel that you have become as skilled as possible and that there is less to be nervous about. That is where the skill lies in becoming professional whenever you are speaking in public or socially.

As mentioned earlier, nervousness is generally caused by lack of practice and by lack of experience – unfortunately somewhat of a 'chicken and egg' situation, but there are clubs that work at giving you such experience and who know that at the beginning many of their members join to improve their style. Your practice can also involve going to public meetings, at the Council Chamber of wherever, and persuading yourself that you are able to get up and communicate without experiencing the problems which you thought you might meet. The advantage of such meetings is that you will be speaking for only a short time and have no need to feel constrained by *having* to fill a period of time which you might feel unable to do. In addition, you can go there secure in the knowledge that no one will know who you are, the reverse of which might otherwise prevent you from speaking at all. It is only practice which will finally convince you that you have a speaking ability but it is certainly practising with rules which are clearly outlined and which need to be followed.

BE AWARE OF YOUR FAULTS – AND CORRECT THEM

Correct and effective conversation become easier the more we become aware that faults are there to be eliminated. Self-confidence comes when we realise that we make fewer mistakes than we did before. The further we go down that road, the less likely we are to be nervous about speaking in the first place, and the higher the probability that we will automatically become more effective simply because our own confidence improves.

As Ralph Waldo Emerson said, 'All good speakers were bad speakers once.' Probably not strictly true but true enough to rely on if you are also aware that you can improve your style to a level of acceptability.

READ AND LISTEN

Sadly, a great number of people who speak badly are unaware of the impression they give to others since it has become trendy, in educational establishments, to neglect the basic reading abilities of those they teach. Consequently we have raised two or three generations who no longer read as a regular part of their lives. Indeed, the actual figures for those who enjoy reading is quoted as down from 45 per cent in the 1940s to under 30 per cent today; an unhappy record when the standards of technical education have risen so rapidly over the same period.

Those who do not read cannot recognise good English since they have not had the opportunity or encouragement to study the style of others. They include engineers who have a university degree in their chosen subject but cannot explain that subject to others, and they include secretaries and the business professionals who cannot create a simple letter without making errors in grammar and punctuation.

The way out of the problem is by reading and listening to others and translating their styles to your own. It is by building your own self-confidence and *knowing* that you have recognised faults and eliminated them from your own work, and it is using that self-confidence to convince others that you are both knowledgeable in your subject and articulate in expressing it. If you hesitate and grope for the right words when you have something to say, if you are unable to carry on a conversation without worrying whether your grammar is right or wrong, and if you are unable to write down your thoughts in a clear and concise way, you are missing out on your chances in life.

Speaking persuasively and with conviction is essentially speaking with self-confidence. Knowledge of what is right will develop that self-confidence and the confidence of others in you. Few were born with their speaking talents and those who speak well also need to develop what talents they have. All your hard work will be rewarded by the knowledge that you can be at home in any environment and at ease with any company. That alone will make all the effort worthwhile.

CHECKLIST

- A good general knowledge is one of the keys to self-confidence.
- Continual practice will eliminate the errors you have.
- To avoid nervousness, you must know that you are in control.
- Be conscious of your errors by listening to others.
- The rewards for good speaking and writing are there for the taking.